Today
God
Says

Today God Says

Daily Reminders of God's Great Love for You

by
CLIFT RICHARDS
with
LLOYD HILDEBRAND·

Victory House, Inc.
Tulsa, Oklahoma

Unless otherwise indicated, all Scripture quotations are taken from the *King James Version* of the Bible.

Today God Says
Copyright © 1997 by K. & C. International, Inc.
ISBN 0-932081-50-9 (Mass-market Paperback)
Published by Victory House, Inc.
P.O. Box 700238
Tulsa, Oklahoma 74170
(918) 747-5009

Printed in the United States of America. All rights reserved under International Copyright Law. Contents and/or cover may not be reproduced in whole or in part, in any form, without the express written consent of the Publisher.

Contents

Books By

CLIFT RICHARDS
——— with ———
LLOYD HILDEBRAND

PRAYERS THAT PREVAIL
(The Believer's Manual of Prayers)

MORE PRAYERS THAT PREVAIL
(Volume 2 of The Believer's Manual of Prayers)

PRAYERS THAT PREVAIL FOR AMERICA
(Changing a Nation Through Prayer)

**PRAYERS THAT PREVAIL FOR
YOUR CHILDREN**
(A Parent's & Grandparent's Manual of Prayers)

A LITTLE BIT OF GOD'S WISDOM AND WIT
*(A Treasury of Quips and Quotes about Life
and Love from God's Infinite Wisdom)*

**A LITTLE BIT OF GOD'S WISDOM & WIT
FOR MEN**
(Gems of Wisdom for Living a Happy and Successful Life)

GOD'S SPECIAL PROMISES TO ME

MINI PRAYERS THAT PREVAIL

TODAY GOD SAYS
(Daily Reminders of God's Great Love for You)

Preface

Today God Says is not a typical devotional book. It is a book of personal messages from God's heart to yours.

There are entries for each day of the year. Each one contains a personal word from God, a promise from His Word, a spiritual meditation, and a scriptural prayer.

Just five minutes every morning with this book will open the windows of heaven into your soul and spirit. You will hear God speaking to *you*.

Your heart will be inspired, your spirits will be lifted, and your faith will be strengthened as this book reminds you of God's love, His promises, and His commitment to you.

Simply reflecting upon His personal assurances to you will change your outlook on each day as you are reminded of what God is saying to *you*:

> *I love you.*
> *You are My child.*
> *I have called you with a holy calling.*
> *I am able to do all things.*
> *You belong to Christ.*
> *My Word will help you grow.*

I am a consuming fire.
I have chosen you.

And a multitude of other personal affirmations from our Father's heart — one for every day of the year. Each one is fortified with personal promises from the Word, such as:

"But seek ye first the kingdom of God, and his righteousness; and all these things shall be added unto you" (Matt. 6:33).

"God is our refuge and strength, a very present help in trouble" (Ps. 46:1).

"Commit thy works unto the Lord, and thy thoughts shall be established" (Prov. 16:3).

Hundreds of other Bible promises are cited throughout the text, and many are reprinted in their entirety. The familiarity and poetic quality of the King James Version enhances our ability to memorize these important truths.

Words of wisdom, including enlightening quotations from various sources, serve to clarify the meaning of the Scriptures in each entry's section entitled: "My response to the Word." These lead to life-giving meditation and contemplation on the Word. Some examples are:

"God's love is not a conditional love;
it is an open-hearted, generous self-giving

which God offers to men. Those who would
carefully limit the operation of God's love
. . . have missed the point" (J.B. Phillips).

"God's love is a fabric that never
fades, no matter how often it is washed
in the waters of adversity and grief"
(Anonymous).

"God never alters the robe of righteousness to fit the man, but the man to fit
the robe" (Anonymous).

In the same way that each daily entry opens
with a personal word from God, it concludes with
a personal prayer to God, based upon the Word.
Many are personalized prayers built directly from
the Scriptures, such as the following:

"Blessed be God, my Father, and the
Father of my Lord Jesus Christ. Thank you,
Lord, for blessing me with every spiritual
blessing in heavenly places with Christ"
(Adapted from Eph. 1).

"Lord, your Word promises me that
you will give me wisdom when I ask for it
in faith, nothing wavering" (Adapted from
James 1:5-6).

By investing only five minutes of your day
in the principles, promises, and prayers of this
book, the focus of your life will change from the

earthly to the spiritual through a step-by-step and day-by-day progression into the life of faith.

You will learn to live the truth of the great promises of the Word, such as this one:

> *"Now unto him that is able to do exceeding abundantly above all that we ask or think, according to the power that worketh in us, Unto him be glory in the church by Christ Jesus throughout all ages, world without end. Amen"* (Eph. 3:20).

You will begin to look forward to each new day, wondering what glorious things God has in store for you, and you will eagerly turn to *Today God Says* in order to learn God's personal word for you.

This book opens the door to an exciting adventure in the Kingdom of God.

January 1

Today God says, *"I love you."*

He promises me: "In this was manifested the love of God toward us, because that God sent his only begotten Son into the world, that we might live through him. Herein is love, not that we loved God, but that he loved us, and sent his Son to be the propitiation [atoning sacrifice] for our sins" (1 John 4:9-10).

My response to the Word: God loves *me*! I receive His love as I reflect on the words of J.B. Phillips who wrote, "God's love is not a conditional love; it is an open-hearted, generous self-giving which God offers to men. Those who would carefully limit the operation of God's love . . . have missed the point."

My prayer: Heavenly Father, thank you for manifesting your love toward me by sending your Son, my Lord and Savior, Jesus Christ, to die for me. His sacrifice for my sins has set me free. Hallelujah! What a Savior!

Today's Scriptures: John 3:16; Rom. 5:8; 1 John 4:18-19.

January 2

Today God says, *"You are My child."*

He promises me: "But as many as received him, to them gave he power to become the sons of God, even to them that believe on his name" (John 1:12).

My response to the Word: I am God's child because I have received Jesus Christ as my personal Savior and Lord. I believe on His wonderful name. It thrills me to know that Almighty God is my Father. His promises are like life preservers. They keep my soul from sinking in the sea of trouble and confusion.

My prayer: Heavenly Father, thank you for adopting me into your family. It is such an honor for me to be your child. With your help, I will be your obedient child throughout this day.

Today's Scriptures: Matt. 6:8; Rom. 8:16; Gal. 3:26; 1 John 3:1-2.

January 3

Today God says, *"Put Me first in your life."*

He promises me: "But seek ye first the kingdom of God, and his righteousness; and all these things shall be added unto you" (Matt. 6:33).

My response to the Word: Throughout this day I will put God first. I will seek His kingdom and His righteousness. I know He will take care of everything else as I obey Him and receive His promises. God's Word declares, "For where your treasure is, there will your heart be also." I want the Lord to be my treasure always. Therefore, I will give God first place in my life.

My prayer: Lord, I will put you first in my life this day. You are the treasure of my heart.

Today's Scriptures: Ps. 16:8; Matt. 6:21; Eph. 1:3; Col. 1:18.

January 4

Today God says, *"My joy is your strength."*

He promises me: ". . . the joy of the Lord is your strength" (Neh. 8:10).

My response to the Word: I will walk in the Lord's joy throughout this day, because I know this is a key to spiritual strength in my life. His joy is not based on circumstances; it is based on truth. I agree with Joseph Marmion who wrote, "Joy is the echo of God's life within us." I believe the Word which tells me that joy is a fruit of the Holy Spirit that dwells within me.

My prayer: Lord, thank you for the wonderful joy you impart to me through your Word and your Spirit. I will let your joy strengthen me for each challenge that comes my way. I will continually rejoice in you, Lord, for you are my joy.

Today's Scriptures: John 15:11; Rom. 5:11; 1 Pet. 1:8.

January 5

Today God says, *"I am your peace."*

He promises me: "The Lord will bless his people with peace" (Ps. 29:11).

My response to the Word: In Christ, I have found a peace that surpasses all understanding. It is a peace that the world cannot give, and neither can the world take it away from me. I remember that Jesus said, "Peace I leave with you, My peace I give to you; not as the world gives do I give to you. Let not your heart be troubled, neither let it be afraid."

My prayer: Lord, thank you for blessing me with your peace through your Word and your Spirit. I believe you have given me your peace. I will walk in your peace throughout this day.

Today's Scriptures: Isa. 26:3; John 14:27; Phil. 4:7; Col. 3:15.

January 6

Today God says, *"You can do all things through Me."*

He promises me: "I can do all things through Christ which strengtheneth me" (Phil. 4:13).

My response to the Word: There is no mountain too high and no valley too low for me to face when I walk in the empowerment God provides for me. I believe the words of Jesus who said, "I am the vine, ye are the branches: He that abideth in me, and I in him, the same bringeth forth much fruit: for without me ye can do nothing."

My prayer: Dear Lord, you enable me to handle every task and challenge of my life. I know that nothing can happen today that you and I cannot handle together. I place my trust in you. I will be strong in you, Lord, and in the power of your might. You are the strength of my heart and my portion forever. Thank you, Master.

Today's Scriptures: Ps. 73:26; Hab. 3:19; John 15:5; 2 Cor. 12:9; Eph. 6:10.

January 7

Today God says, *"I know all your needs."*

He promises me: "Your Father knoweth what things ye have need of, before ye ask him" (Matt. 6:8).

My response to the Word: I know that my heavenly Father knows everything about me. He knows what I need, and He promises to meet my needs. The Word of God says, "But my God shall supply all your need according to his riches in glory by Christ Jesus."

My prayer: Thank you, Lord, for your amazing love that always seeks to meet my needs. I pray in faith, realizing that you are able to do all things and that all the promises of your Word are true, and they are for *me*.

Today's Scriptures: Phil. 4:19; Heb. 4:16; Heb. 10:36.

January 8

Today God says, *"I care about you."*

He promises me: "Casting all your care upon him; for he careth for you" (1 Pet. 5:7).

My response to the Word: I never need to worry about anything because God has invited me to cast all my cares upon Him. I do so now, and I believe with all my heart that He will handle everything in the best possible way. Every day has two handles available — the handle of anxiety and the handle of faith. I take hold of this day with the handle of faith.

My prayer: Father in heaven, thank you for your invitation to cast all my worries and cares upon you. I do this now through the faith your Word imparts to me. I know you take good care of your children. As your beloved child I trust you to take care of me.

Today's Scriptures: 1 John 3:1; 1 John 4:7; 1 John 5:3.

January 9

Today God says, *"I will never leave you."*

He promises me: "I will never leave thee, nor forsake thee" (Heb. 13:5).

My response to the Word: God's presence is the environment of my life. "For in him we live, and move, and have our being." I will practice His presence throughout this day as I continue to abide in Him. I claim the prayer promise that Jesus stated so clearly: "If ye abide in me, and my words abide in you, ye shall ask what ye will, and it shall be done unto you." I believe the Scripture that tells me that I am a temple of the Holy Spirit. God dwells in me. Greater is He that is in me than he that is in the world.

My prayer: Lord, I thank you for your presence which cheers me, strengthens me, and guides me. I know you will never leave me nor forsake me. I will abide in you throughout this day.

Today's Scriptures: Matt. 28:20; John 15:7; Acts 17:28; 1 Cor. 6:19; 1 John 4:4.

January 10

Today God says, *"I give My wisdom to you."*

He promises me: "If any of you lack wisdom, let him ask of God, that giveth to all men liberally, and upbraideth not; and it shall be given him. But let him ask in faith, nothing wavering" (James 1:5-6).

My response to the Word: The wisdom of God is available to me through faith-filled praying. Whenever a situation arises that requires insights from God, He invites me to ask Him for the wisdom that only He can give. I will seek His wisdom throughout this day, and I will walk in the wisdom He imparts to me. I receive His wisdom through faith as I apply His Word to my life and claim His promises through prayer.

My prayer: God, you are my wisdom. Your Word and your Spirit give me insights into your wisdom. I will be led by your Spirit and I will walk in the wisdom and truth of your Word throughout this day. Thank you for your wisdom, Father.

Today's Scriptures: Prov. 24:3; Acts 6:3; Eph. 1:8; Col. 4:5.

January 11

Today God says, *"I am the Light of the world."*

He promises me: "Ye are the light of the world. . . . Let your light so shine before men, that they may see your good works, and glorify your Father which is in heaven" (Matt. 5:14-16).

My response to the Word: Jesus is the Light of the world, and He says that I am the light of the world as well. He wants me to let my light shine in this world of darkness by doing good works so that others will glorify my heavenly Father. I will let the light of Jesus Christ shine through my life throughout this day by doing good works in His name. I will walk continually in the light of God's Word and in the sunlight of God's love.

My prayer: Father of lights, with whom there is no change, I thank you for translating me from this world of darkness, into your marvelous light. Thank you for your Word which gives me light. I will walk in your light throughout this day.

Today's Scriptures: Ps. 119:130; John 1:9; John 8:12; 1 Pet. 2:9; 1 John 1:7.

January 12

Today God says, *"I give you abundant life."*

He promises me: "I am come that they might have life, and that they might have it more abundantly" (John 10:10).

My response to the Word: An abundant life is one that is filled with good things — health, prosperity, spiritual blessings, peace, joy, love, etc. I receive Jesus' promise of abundance in my life this day. I believe He wants me to walk in the abundance He provides for me. Paul wrote, "Blessed be the God and Father of our Lord Jesus Christ, who hath blessed us with all spiritual blessings in heavenly places in Christ."

My prayer: Blessed be God, my Father, and the Father of my Lord Jesus Christ. Thank you, Lord, for blessing *me* with every spiritual blessing in heavenly places with Christ. Thank you for giving me abundant life.

Today's Scriptures: Eph. 1:3; Eph. 3:20; Titus 3:6.

January 13

Today God says, *"I am the door."*

He promises me: "Verily, verily, I say unto you, I am the door of the sheep" (John 10:7).

My response to the Word: Jesus is the doorway into a new dimension — a higher dimension of living — for *me.* He wants *me* — His sheep — to go through the door, into His green pastures of rest and provision. I accept His offer, and I walk through the door, realizing that the Lord is my Shepherd, therefore, "I shall not want. He maketh me to lie down in green pastures: he leadeth me beside the still waters. He restoreth my soul: he leadeth me in the paths of righteousness for his name's sake."

My prayer: Lord, thank you for shepherding me. I choose to lie down in the green pastures you have provided for me. Thank you for leading me beside the still waters, and for restoring my soul. I will walk in the paths of righteousness for your name's sake.

Today's Scriptures: Ps. 23:1-3; John 10:9; John 14:6.

January 14

Today God says, *"Abide in Me, and let My words abide in you."*

He promises me: "If ye abide in me, and my words abide in you, ye shall ask what ye will, and it shall be done unto you" (John 15:7).

My response to the Word: I will abide in Christ and I will let the Word of God sink deep within my soul and spirit. By so doing I know that God will hear and answer my prayers. Wonderful things will happen to me as I live expectantly, believe confidently, and pray affirmatively. I will constantly abide in Jesus Christ, my Lord.

My prayer: Lord, I am a branch and you are the vine. In order to be a fruitful branch I know I must stay close to you, abide in your presence, and let your words abide in me. This gives me faith, rest, and hope, and it brings answers to my prayers. Thank you for letting me abide in you. Thank you for your Word.

Today's Scriptures: John 5:38-40; 1 John 2:28; 1 John 3:6.

January 15

Today God says, *"Trust in Me with all your heart."*

He promises me: "Trust in the Lord with all thine heart; and lean not unto thine own understanding.

In all thy ways acknowledge him, and he shall direct thy paths" (Prov. 3:5-6).

My response to the Word: I know God is trustworthy. He is always faithful. I will trust Him with all my heart and acknowledge Him in all my ways. He will direct me throughout this day. It is such an adventure to be led by the Spirit of God! I am glad to be a child of God.

My prayer: Heavenly Father, I trust in you. I want to learn to trust you with all my heart, to acknowledge your presence, and experience your direction in my life each step of my way. Thank you for your wonderful promise that you will guide me, lead me, direct me, and be with me.

Today's Scriptures: Prov. 28:25; 1 Tim. 4:10; 1 Tim. 6:17.

January 16

Today God says, *"All things in your life work together for good for you."*

He promises me: "And we know that all things work together for good to them that love God, to them who are the called according to his purpose" (Rom. 8:28).

My response to the Word: God is weaving a beautiful tapestry with the threads of my life. He sees the complete picture; I see only a part of it, but I know that He'll put the pieces together in a marvelous way because I love Him and He has called me. This gives my life purpose and meaning. I am comforted because I know the Holy Spirit is praying and interceding for me.

My prayer: Heavenly Father, thank you for the great and precious promises of your Word that provide me with faith, hope, and wisdom. I thank you that I can truly believe that you are causing all things to work together for good in my life according to your will.

Today's Scriptures: Eph. 1:11; Phil. 4:13; Col. 1:18.

January 17

Today God says, *"I am the way."*

He promises me: "I am the way, the truth, and the life: no man cometh unto the Father, but by me" (John 14:6).

My response to the Word: Jesus is the way, the truth, and the life. I will follow no other way. Through Him I have access to my Father in heaven. The truth of Jesus Christ has made me free. He has given me abundant life. He has made me new.

My prayer: Heavenly Father, thank you for sending Jesus Christ to live and die for me. Through Him, I am able to pray with confidence and to come boldly to your throne of grace. I will live according to His way, His truth, and His life.

Today's Scriptures: John 8:32; John 10:10; 1 Cor. 5:17; Heb. 4:16; Heb. 10:19.

January 18

Today God says, *"You shall be My witness."*

He promises me: "But ye shall receive power, after that the Holy Ghost is come upon you: and ye shall be witnesses unto me both in Jerusalem, and in all Judaea, and in Samaria, and unto the uttermost part of the earth" (Acts 1:8).

My response to the Word: I will be a faithful witness for my Lord and Savior Jesus Christ throughout this day. His Spirit empowers me to help to fulfill the Great Commission. I will share the Gospel of Jesus Christ with other people throughout this day. I will remember that every person I meet today is either a missionary or a mission field. Everyone I see needs either to know you or to know you better.

My prayer: Lord, fill me with your Spirit and empower me to be your faithful witness today. Lead me to those who need to hear about your saving grace.

Today's Scriptures: Matt. 28:19-20; Rom. 1:16; 2 Cor. 5:20.

January 19

Today God says, *"I am a very present help in times of trouble."*

He promises me: "God is our refuge and strength, a very present help in trouble" (Ps. 46:1).

My response to the Word: God is the rock of my strength. He is my refuge and my fortress. I place all of my trust in Him. My God is a very present help to me. He never leaves me nor forsakes me. He is the God who is always there.

My prayer: Lord God, you are my refuge and my strength. You are with me. I will abide in the safety of your loving presence throughout this day.

Today's Scriptures: Ps. 33:20; Ps. 62:7; Heb. 4:16; Heb. 13:5.

January 20

Today God says, *"You are more than a conqueror."*

He promises me: "Nay, in all these things we are more than conquerors through him that loved us" (Rom. 8:37).

My response to the Word: I am more than a conqueror through Jesus Christ. I can do all things through Him. Without Him, I can do nothing. Throughout this day I will remember that God doesn't call me to be successful, according to the standards of this world, but He does call me to be faithful (full of faith). He will take care of the rest. I am an overcomer, because greater is He that is in me than he that is in the world.

My prayer: Loving Lord, I give my life to you afresh. Throughout this day I realize that I will prevail against all obstacles and foes because you have told me that I am more than a conqueror through Christ. I believe your Word. Help me to be strong in you, Lord, and in the power of your might.

Today's Scriptures: John 15:5; Eph. 6:10; Phil. 4:13; 1 John 4:4; 1 John 5:4.

January 21

Today God says, *"I am your Shepherd."*

He promises me: "The Lord is my shepherd; I shall not want" (Ps. 23:1).

My response to the Word: Because the Lord is my Shepherd, I will never lack any good thing. He will supply all my needs according to His riches in glory through Christ Jesus. He will lead me, guide me, nurture me, protect me, keep me, feed me, and love me. Jesus Christ is the Good Shepherd of my life.

My prayer: Lord, you are my Shepherd. I am so happy to be a sheep in your flock. Thank you for guiding me, protecting me, and feeding me. Thank you for giving your life for me.

Today's Scriptures: John 10:11; Phil. 4:19; Heb. 13:20.

January 22

Today God says, *"Goodness and mercy will follow you forever."*

He promises me: "Surely goodness and mercy shall follow me all the days of my life: and I will dwell in the house of the Lord for ever" (Ps. 23:6).

My response to the Word: God's goodness and mercy have always been with me, even when I didn't realize it. His mercy is everlasting. I will walk in His goodness and mercy throughout this day, and I know the future will be wonderful because I will dwell in the Lord's house forever!

My prayer: Lord, thank you for your goodness and mercy. As I go forth in your love today, I know they will follow me. It is so wonderful to know that I will be with you forever. You are so wonderful, Father. Please give me more revelation of your goodness and mercy.

Today's Scriptures: Ps. 108:4; Prov. 3:3; Eph. 2:4.

January 23

Today God says, *"You have eternal life."*

He promises me: "For the wages of sin is death; but the gift of God is eternal life through Jesus Christ our Lord" (Rom. 6:23).

My response to the Word: The stunning knowledge that eternal life has been given to me by my loving Father in heaven leads me into perpetual thankfulness for having received what I did not deserve (eternal life), and for not receiving what I did deserve (death). Because I've been born twice, I will have to die only once.

My prayer: Dear Father, thank you for your amazing grace that gives me eternal life with you. Through faith in your Son I have been set free from the wages of sin. I will live for you.

Today's Scriptures: John 3:3; John 3:16; 1 John 5:13.

January 24

Today God says, *"I hear your prayers."*

He promises me: "And this is the confidence that we have in him, that, if we ask any thing according to his will, he heareth us" (1 John 5:14).

My response to the Word: God hears me when I pray if I pray according to His will. His will is revealed in His Word. Therefore, I will pray according to the Word of God. In this way I can be assured at all times that I am praying His will and He is hearing my prayers. "And if we know that he hear us, whatsoever we ask, we know that we have the petitions that we desired of him."

My prayer: Father, it is so good to know that you want me to express my needs to you in prayer. I believe your Word which invites me, "Call unto me, and I will answer thee, and shew thee great and mighty things, which thou knowest not." Thank you, Father.

Today's Scriptures: Jer. 33:3; Dan. 9:19; 1 John 5:15.

January 25

Today God says, *"Whatever you do will prosper."*

He promises me: "And he shall be like a tree planted by the rivers of water, that bringeth forth his fruit in his season; his leaf also shall not wither; and whatsoever he doeth shall prosper" (Ps. 1:3).

My response to the Word: I will delight in the Word of God throughout this day. This will make my time fruitful and it will assure prosperity in my life. I will not walk in the counsel of the ungodly, nor stand in the way of sinners. Instead, I will meditate upon God's precious Word throughout this day.

My prayer: Father, thank you for your Word. I love its practical truths which guide my life. Your Word is a lamp unto my feet and a light unto my path. I will adhere to your Word today, and I know you will make my way prosperous. Fill me with your Spirit so that I will produce the fruit of your Spirit in all my relationships and responsibilities. I will give your Word first place in my life today.

Today's Scriptures: Deut. 29:9; Ps. 122:6; 3 John 2.

January 26

Today God says, *"I am your defense."*

He promises me: "My defence is of God, which saveth the upright in heart" (Ps. 7:10).

My response to the Word: I surrender my right to self-defense because I know God will defend me in a far better way than I ever could. I will walk in uprightness of heart throughout this day, and I know God will save me from my enemies. I belong to the Lord, and I know He always takes good care of His children!

My prayer: Thank you, Lord God, for protecting me and defending me against the forces of evil and wickedness in the world. I will fear no evil, because I know you are with me.

Today's Scriptures: Ps. 23:4; Ps. 59:9; Ps. 94:22.

January 27

Today God says, *"You shall not be moved."*

He promises me: "I have set the Lord always before me: because he is at my right hand, I shall not be moved" (Ps. 16:8).

My response to the Word: I will keep focused on the Lord throughout this day. I will see Him at my right hand. I will keep looking unto Jesus who is "the author and finisher of our faith," as I lay aside every weight, and all besetting sins. I will run with patience the race that is set before me.

My prayer: Lord, your keeping power is always at work in my life as I keep my mind stayed upon you. You are the Author and Finisher of my faith and I will keep focused on you as I go about my daily duties.

Today's Scriptures: Ps. 30:6; Ps. 62:6; Ps. 121:3; Heb. 12:1-2.

January 28

Today God says, *"I am your Lord."*

He promises me: "The Lord is the portion of mine inheritance and of my cup: thou maintainest my lot" (Ps. 16:5).

My response to the Word: I surrender all my rights and possessions, indeed my very life, to the Lord. He is my Master; I am His servant. By yielding every part of my life to Him, I find true freedom — the "glorious liberty of the children of God." It is a privilege and an honor to be a servant of the Lord.

My prayer: Lord, I give you complete control of every area of my life. I truly surrender all to you. Thank you for the peace and freedom this gives to me.

Today's Scriptures: Ps. 23:1; Rom. 8:21; Eph. 4:5.

January 29

Today God says, *"Your labor is never in vain when you work for Me."*

He promises me: "Therefore, my beloved brethren, be ye stedfast, unmoveable, always abounding in the work of the Lord, forasmuch as ye know that your labour is not in vain in the Lord" (1 Cor. 15:58).

My response to the Word: Throughout this day I will endeavor to be steadfast and unmoveable as I abound in the work of the Lord. I know that my labor will never be in vain when I work for the Lord, in His perfect way. I will remember that the Lord didn't burden me with work; He blessed me with it.

My prayer: Loving Lord, I am thankful for every opportunity you give me to serve you. I know you will enable me to do everything you call me to do. Thank you for your power that equips me to work for you.

Today's Scriptures: Luke 4:8; Rom. 7:6; Rom. 12:11.

January 30

Today God says, *"I am your Deliverer."*

He promises me: "The Lord is my rock, and my fortress, and my deliverer; my God, my strength, in whom I will trust; my buckler, and the horn of my salvation, and my high tower. I will call upon the Lord, who is worthy to be praised: so shall I be saved from mine enemies" (Ps. 18:2-3).

My response to the Word: God delivers me from all my enemies. When He delivers me, I am completely free. Therefore, I will call upon Him throughout this day because I know He is my rock, my fortress, my Deliverer, my buckler, the horn of my salvation, and my high tower. He is worthy to be praised, and I will praise Him throughout this day.

My prayer: Lord, I praise you and thank you for saving me from all my enemies. I thank you also that I have been completely delivered from all guilt, condemnation, fear, sin, shame, and opposition. You are my mighty Deliverer. I love you, Lord. Thank you for loving me.

Today's Scriptures: Ps. 51:14; 2 Tim. 4:18; 2 Pet. 2:9.

January 31

Today God says, "I will show you the path of life."

He promises me, "Thou wilt shew me the path of life: in thy presence is fulness of joy; at thy right hand there are pleasures for evermore" (Ps. 16:11).

My response to the Word: Through His Word God has shown me the path of life. I will walk in His paths throughout this day. As I do so, even now, I am experiencing the fulness of joy that He promises to me, and I know I will be able to enjoy His pleasures forevermore. My heart is filled with thanksgiving as I meditate upon these wondrous truths.

My prayer: Father in heaven, thank you for revealing the path of life to me. "Thy word is a lamp unto my feet, and a light unto my path." I will walk in the light of your Word throughout this day.

Today's Scriptures: Ps. 119:105; John 10:10; Col. 3:3; 2 Tim. 1:1.

February 1

Today God says, *"You are the apple of My eye."*

He promises me: "Keep me as the apple of the eye, hide me under the shadow of thy wings" (Ps. 17:8).

My response to the Word: God is keeping me as the apple of His eye, and He is hiding me under the shadow of His wings. "I will say of the Lord, He is my refuge and my fortress: my God; in him will I trust." He will cover me with His feathers, and under His wings I will trust. His truth will be my shield and buckler.

My prayer: Lord, thank you for protecting me and defending me from all harm. I will stay in the safe place you have provided for me, beneath the shadow of your wings, within the shelter of your presence.

Today's Scriptures: Ps. 63:3; Ps. 91:2; Ps. 91:4.

February 2

Today God says, *"I will answer your prayers."*

He promises me: "He shall call upon me, and I will answer him: I will be with him in trouble; I will deliver him, and honour him" (Ps. 91:15).

My response to the Word: I know the Lord hears me when I call to Him in prayer. I know

He wants me to pray and to seek His face. He promises me that He will answer my prayers if I use the keys to answered prayer He has provided for me in His Word. Throughout this day I will remember that if I get too busy to pray, I am too busy. I will pray without ceasing.

My prayer: Lord God, thank you for the direct access to you that prayer provides for me. I love to pray and to seek your face, and I will pray without ceasing throughout this day, realizing that you will answer my prayers when I pray according to your will as it is revealed in your Word.

Today's Scriptures: Matt. 21:22; 1 Thess. 5:17; 1 Pet. 3:12; 1 Pet. 4:7.

February 3

Today God says, *"I will gird you with strength."*

He promises me: "For who is God save the Lord? or who is a rock save our God? It is God that girdeth me with strength, and maketh my way perfect" (Ps. 18:31-32).

My response to the Word: God girds me with strength and He makes my way perfect, because He is "a buckler to all those that trust in him." He enables me to "run through a troop; and by my God have I leaped over a wall. As for God, his way is perfect." He is girding me with strength for this very day and, "He maketh my feet like hinds' feet, and setteth me upon my high places." I love the Lord.

My prayer: Lord God, thank you for girding me with strength and enabling me to face every challenge and difficulty that comes my way. I will walk in your strength throughout this day.

Today's Scriptures: Ps. 18:29; Ps. 18:30; Ps. 18:33.

February 4

Today God says, *"The heavens declare My glory."*

He promises me: "The heavens declare the glory of God; and the firmament sheweth his handywork" (Ps. 19:1).

My response to the Word: When I take the time to look at the spectacular creation that is all around me I see the glory of God. The beauty of the heavens and the earth is a true testimony of God's power, grace, and glory. As I realize that He created this wonderful environment for me to enjoy, my heart is filled with gratitude for the mountains, the sky, the clouds, the rainbow, the rivers, the seas, the lakes, the flowers, the trees, the wildlife, and all the beauty of this earth. Thank you, Father.

My prayer: Father, help me to truly see the declaration of your glory in the heavens and the earth. Your creative power is truly awesome, and

I will reflect upon your handywork throughout this day. Thank you, Lord.

Today's Scriptures: Rom. 1:20; Col. 1:16; Rev. 4:11.

February 5

Today God says, *"Let my peace rule in your heart."*

He promises me: "And let the peace of God rule in your hearts, to the which also ye are called in one body; and be ye thankful" (Col. 3:15).

My response to the Word: I will let God's peace rule in my heart throughout this day. Peace of heart and peace of mind are precious treasures, and I will let nothing disturb my peace. Jesus said, "Peace I leave with you, my peace I give unto you: not as the world giveth, give I unto you. Let not your heart be troubled, neither let it be afraid."

My prayer: Lord, I treasure the peace you have imparted to me. The world can't give me peace, and it can't take it away from me. My heart is truly thankful for your peace, and I will walk in your peace throughout this day.

Today's Scriptures: Isa. 26:3; John 14:27; Eph. 2:14.

February 6

Today God says, *"I am your Father."*

He promises me: "Your Father knoweth what things ye have need of, before ye ask him" (Matt. 6:8).

My response to the Word: When God, my heavenly Father, makes a promise, I respond with faith. Faith believes His promises, hope anticipates the fulfillment of His promises, and patience quietly waits for the manifestation. My safe place is in the lap of my Father where I know all my needs will be met.

My prayer: Heavenly Father, I love you with all my heart. I know you care about me, and I know you want to meet my needs. I receive your love right now as I pray. I ask for greater understanding of your fatherly love for me Thank you, Father.

Today's Scriptures: Luke 11:2; John 15:16; 1 John 1:2-3.

February 7

Today God says, *"I am able to do all things."*

He promises me: "Now unto him that is able to do exceeding abundantly above all that we ask or think, according to the power that worketh in us" (Eph. 3:20).

My response to the Word: God has absolutely no limitations. With Him, all things are possible. The only thing He can't do is fail. In fact, He is able

to do "exceeding abundantly above all" that I can
ask or think. Therefore, I will not hesitate to ask
my heavenly Father to meet my needs. He wants
to do so, and He will do so in ways that go
beyond my level of anticipation.

My prayer: Almighty God, you are able to do
all things. You are my miracle-working Father. I
ask you now for the following: _____

_____

_____.

Today's Scriptures: Matt. 19:26; Col. 1:17; Col. 1:19.

February 8

Today God says, "*I am faithful to you.*"

He promises me: "It is of the Lord's mercies
that we are not consumed, because his compassions
fail not. They are new every morning: great is thy
faithfulness. The Lord is my portion, saith my
soul; therefore will I hope in him. The Lord is
good unto them that wait for him, to the soul that
seeketh him" (Lam. 3:22-25).

My response to the Word: God is always faithful
to His Word. He will never allow anything to
come to me that He and I can't handle together.
He keeps all the promises of His Word. He says,
"So shall my word be that goeth forth out of my
mouth: it shall not return unto me void, but it

shall accomplish that which I please, and it shall prosper in the thing whereto I sent it."

My prayer: Father in heaven, thank you for your great faithfulness which is new every morning of my life. I believe all the promises of your Word. I know you will never let me down.

Today's Scriptures: Isa. 55:11; 1 Thess. 5:24; 2 Thess. 3:3.

February 9

Today God says, *"You are the salt of the earth."*

He promises me: "Ye are the salt of the earth: but if the salt have lost his savour, wherewith shall it be salted? it is thenceforth good for nothing, but to be cast out, and to be trodden under foot of men" (Matt. 5:13).

My response to the Word: When I think of salt, I think of its thirst-producing and flavor-enhancing qualities. I want to be like salt in that I want to make other people thirsty for Jesus, and I want to make life more flavorful and tasty for others. Jesus calls me "the salt of the earth," and I will be careful to maintain the flavor of salt through His Word, prayer, Christian fellowship, and worship so that others will be able to: ". . . taste and see that the Lord is good."

My prayer: Dear Lord, I thank you for the personal affirmation you've given to me — that I am the salt of the earth. I will make every effort today to be a "salty" Christian. Help me, Father, to be full of flavor, healing, and love in all my relationships.

Today's Scriptures: Ps. 34:8; Mark 9:50; Luke 14:34.

February 10

Today God says, *"You are the light of the world."*

He promises me: "Ye are the light of the world. A city that is set on an hill cannot be hid. Neither do men light a candle, and put it under a bushel, but on a candlestick; and it giveth light unto all that are in the house. Let your light so shine before men, that they may see your good works, and glorify your Father which is in heaven" (Matt. 5:14-16).

My response to the Word: I am the light of the world, illuminated by the abiding Light of Jesus Christ who lives within me. Throughout this day I will let His light shine through me. Wherever I go, I will dispel the darkness of this world. I will do good works at every opportunity that is presented to me. In this way, I know that others will glorify my Father in heaven.

My prayer: Father, thank you for Jesus Christ who is the Light of the world. Help me to be like Him, allowing my light to shine wherever I go. I want others to see you in my life today.

Today's Scriptures: John 12:36; Eph. 5:8; 1 Thess. 5:5.

February 11

Today God says, *"Love your enemies."*

He promises me: "Love your enemies, bless them that curse you, do good to them that hate you, and pray for them which despitefully use you, and persecute you; That ye may be the children of your Father which is in heaven" (Matt. 5:44-45).

My response to the Word: Throughout this day I will obey my Lord and Savior, Jesus Christ, by loving my enemies, blessing those who curse me, doing good to those who hate me, and praying for those who despitefully use me and persecute me. This is the life-style of a child of God. It is my choice to respond in positive ways when others oppose me. This is my commitment to my Father in heaven.

My prayer: Lord, your Word tells me that I can expect persecution in this world. Help me to be your faithful witness in times of tribulation and persecution by responding in your way at all times.

Today's Scriptures: Luke 6:27; John 16:33; 1 Cor. 15:25.

February 12

Today God says, *"Pray without ceasing."*

He promises me: "See that none render evil for evil unto any man; but ever follow that which is good, both among yourselves, and to all men. Rejoice evermore. Pray without ceasing. In every thing give thanks: for this is the will of God in Christ Jesus concerning you" (1 Thess. 5:15-18).

My response to the Word: Prayer is my life-line. I will pray without ceasing throughout this day. Through the power of prayer I will be able to follow that which is good, to rejoice at all times, and to give thanks in everything. This is my Father's will for me, and He wants me to follow these principles because He knows it will be good for me.

My prayer: Thank you, Father, for the practical advice your Word provides for me in matters of daily living. I will live according to those principles today. With your help, I will keep on keeping on through faith, rejoicing, incessant prayer, and thanksgiving.

Today's Scriptures: 1 Cor. 7:5; Eph. 6:18; 1 Thess. 5:17.

February 13

Today God says, *"Godliness with contentment is great gain for you."*

He promises me: "But godliness with contentment is great gain. For we brought nothing into this world, and it is certain we can carry nothing out. And having food and raiment let us be therewith content" (1 Tim. 6:6-8).

My response to the Word: Paul wrote, "Not that I speak in respect of want: for I have learned in whatsoever state I am, therewith to be content." With God's help, I will walk in contentment throughout this day, realizing that God will supply all of my needs according to His riches in glory by Christ Jesus. I know that a contented mind is one of God's greatest blessings.

My prayer: Dear Father, thank you for the blessing of contentment I now enjoy as I place all my trust in you. Help me to maintain an attitude of contentment throughout this day.

Today's Scriptures: Isa. 58:11; Phil. 4:11-13; Phil. 4:19; Heb. 13:5.

February 14

Today God says, *"You are being filled with the fruits of righteousness."*

He promises me: "That ye may approve things that are excellent; that ye may be sincere and without offence till the day of Christ; Being filled with the fruits of righteousness, which are by Jesus Christ, unto the glory and praise of God" (Phil. 1:10-11).

My response to the Word: I am being filled with the fruits of righteousness which Jesus Christ imparts to me through faith. I will wear the garments of righteousness throughout this day, realizing that God doesn't alter the robe of righteousness to fit me, but he alters me so that I will fit into the robe.

My prayer: Heavenly Father, thank you for fitting me for the robes of righteousness. I will greatly rejoice in you throughout this day. My soul will be joyful in you. Thank you for filling me with the fruits of righteousness.

Today's Scriptures: Isa. 61:10; Matt. 7:20; Phil. 1:11.

February 15

Today God says, *"My glory is upon you."*

He promises me: "Arise, shine: for thy light is come, and the glory of the Lord is risen upon thee" (Isa. 60:1).

My response to the Word: As I arise with joy today, I realize that the light of the Lord is shining upon me. I will walk in the sunlight of His love throughout this day, and I will walk in the glory of God which has risen upon me. His cloud of glory is the very atmosphere of my life. In Him I live and move and have my being.

My prayer: Thank you for your glory, Father, which fills my soul and surrounds me as I go about my daily activities. I want to take your glory wherever I go so that others will be drawn to you.

Today's Scriptures: Acts 17:28; Eph. 3:21; Col. 1:27.

February 16

Today God says, *"I have anointed you."*

He promises me, "The Spirit of the Lord God is upon me; because the Lord hath anointed me to preach good tidings unto the meek; he hath sent me to bind up the brokenhearted, to proclaim liberty to the captives, and the opening of the prison to them that are bound; To proclaim the acceptable year of the Lord, and the day of vengeance of our God; to comfort all that mourn; To appoint them that mourn in Zion, to give unto them beauty for ashes, the oil of joy for mourning, the garment of praise for the spirit of heaviness; that they might be called trees of righteousness, the planting of the Lord, that he might be glorified" (Isa. 61:1-3).

My response to the Word: The Anointed One
— Jesus of Nazareth — lives within me. Therefore,
the anointing God put upon Him is within me. I
will let His anointing arise and cover me as I go
forth to serve Him. He will lead me to the meek,
the broken-hearted, the captives, the bound, those
in mourning, and those in depression so that I can
help them receive beauty for their ashes, the oil of
joy for their mourning, and the garment of praise
for the spirit of heaviness.

My prayer: Lead me, Lord, to those who
will receive healing and freedom through your
anointing this day. Prepare their hearts for your
deliverance. Help me to be a faithful, anointed
witness to each one.

Today's Scriptures: Ps. 45:7; 2 Cor. 1:21; Heb.
1:9; 1 John 2:20,27.

February 17

Today God says, *"I have redeemed you."*

He promises me: "O give thanks unto the Lord,
for he is good: for his mercy endureth for ever.
Let the redeemed of the Lord say so, whom he hath
redeemed from the hand of the enemy" (Ps. 107:1-2).

My response to the Word: Jesus Christ is my
Redeemer. He has set me free from the hand of
the enemy. I will give thanks to Him throughout
this day, and I will be sure to tell others about His

redemption. Through His blood He bought me
back from the control of Satan and set me free to
serve Him. This I will do with all my heart and
strength throughout this day.

My prayer: Father in heaven, thank you for
sending Jesus to be my Redeemer. I now realize
that I am not my own any longer. Jesus is my
Lord; I am your child. I rejoice as I say "I am
redeemed." Use me in your service, I pray.

Today's Scriptures: Job 19:25; Ps. 19:14; Prov.
23:11; 1 Cor. 6:20.

February 18

Today God says, "*I will satisfy your longing soul.*"

He promises me: "Oh that men would praise
the Lord for his goodness, and for his wonderful
works to the children of men! For he satisfieth the
longing soul, and filleth the hungry soul with
goodness" (Ps. 107:8-9).

My response to the Word: God has performed
a multitude of wonderful works in my life. I
thank Him and praise Him for all He has done,
and I worship Him for who He is in my life. He
truly has satisfied my longing soul and he has
filled my hungry soul with goodness. Throughout
this day, therefore, I will praise my Lord. I will
worship and adore Him for He is so good to me.

My prayer: Thank you, Lord, for satisfying my longing soul and for satisfying my spiritual hunger and thirst. You are my life — you are my everything.

Today's Scriptures: Ps. 91:16; Ps. 132:15; Isa. 58:11.

February 19

Today God says, *"Commit your works to me."*

He promises me: "Commit thy works unto the Lord, and thy thoughts shall be established" (Prov. 16:3).

My response to the Word: I want my thoughts to be established throughout this day. I do not want to be double-minded or inconsistent in any way. I want to serve the Lord in single-minded devotion. He has shown me how to find such consistency and constancy in my thoughts — by committing my works to Him. This I will do each step of the way.

My prayer: Loving Lord, I commit my way and my works to you. Whatever I do this day, I will do as unto you. In so doing, I know you will establish my thoughts, and you will keep my mind from wandering so that I will be a fruitful believer. Thank you, Father.

Today's Scriptures: Ps. 37:5; Prov. 3:5-6; Rom. 12:1-2.

February 20

Today God says, *"I am your salvation."*

He promises me: "Behold, God is my salvation; I will trust, and not be afraid: for the Lord Jehovah is my strength and my song; he also is become my salvation" (Isa. 12:2).

My response to the Word: God is my salvation. I will trust Him and not be afraid. He is my strength and my song. Realizing these marvelous facts, I will trust in the Lord with all my heart. I will stop leaning to my own understanding. Instead, I will lean upon him. In all my ways I will acknowledge Him, and I know He will direct my paths.

My prayer: Lord, thank you for saving me when I came to you through faith. By grace through faith you saved me. Thank you for such a wonderful gift.

Today's Scriptures: Prov. 3:5-6; Jon. 2:9; Acts 4:12.

February 21

Today God says, *"I have already blessed you with every spiritual blessing."*

He promises me: "Blessed be the God, and Father of our Lord Jesus Christ, who hath blessed us with all spiritual blessings in heavenly places in Christ" (Eph. 1:3).

My response to the Word: All spiritual blessings in heavenly places in Christ are already mine! All spiritual blessings have already been given to me! Every single one! Such knowledge amazes me, and it leads me to praise my heavenly Father at all times. Blessed be God, the Father of my Lord Jesus Christ.

My prayer: Thank you, Father, for blessing me with all spiritual blessings in Christ, and for seating me with Him in the heavenly places. I will bless you and thank you throughout this day.

Today's Scriptures: Deut. 28:2; Prov. 10:6; Eph. 2:6.

February 22

Today God says, *"Judge not, and you shall not be judged."*

He promises me: "Judge not, and ye shall not be judged: condemn not, and ye shall not be condemned: forgive, and ye shall be forgiven" (Luke 6:37).

My response to the Word: I will not judge or condemn other people. Instead, I will forgive those who do wrong, especially those who wrong me. As I do this, I know God will not judge me or condemn me, and as I practice forgiveness in my life, I know He will forgive me. Forgiveness is a key that unlocks the door of resentment and the handcuffs of hate. It is a power that breaks the chains of bitterness and the shackles of selfishness.

My prayer: Heavenly Father, help me to avoid the pitfalls and traps that have the power to ensnare one who judges and condemns others. Help me to practice forgiveness throughout this day. Help me to show mercy to others rather than being critical. Thank you, Lord, for the promises of your Word.

Today's Scriptures: Matt. 6:14; Mark 11:25; Gal. 6:1.

February 23

Today God says, *"Give, and it shall be given unto you."*

He promises me: "Give, and it shall be given unto you; good measure, pressed down, and shaken together, and running over, shall men give into your bosom. For with the same measure that ye mete withal it shall be measured to you again" (Luke 6:38).

My response to the Word: I will give to God and others at every possible opportunity throughout this day. God promises that the more I give, the more I receive. This is an amazing truth. I realize that this is very different from the way the world thinks. But the Scripture tells me that obedient giving brings God's blessing. As I give, I am planting seeds that will bring forth a harvest. Two marks of a Christian (both stemming from love) are giving and forgiving.

My prayer: Heavenly Father, you have given so much to me. Thank you for all the blessings I've received. I desire to give as much as possible of my time, my talents, my possessions, my money, and my love throughout this day. Help me to be a faithful steward of all you've given to me.

Today's Scriptures: Mal. 3:10; Matt. 10:8; 2 Cor. 9:7.

February 24

Today God says, *"You shall receive the reward of your inheritance."*

He promises me: "And whatsoever ye do, do it heartily, as to the Lord, and not unto men; Knowing that of the Lord ye shall receive the reward of the inheritance: for ye serve the Lord Christ" (Col. 3:23-24).

My response to the Word: I will face many responsibilities throughout this day. I will remember that a good definition of "responsibility" is "my response to God's ability." I will approach everything I do today with the idea that I am doing it unto God and for God. He promises me that I will receive a wonderful inheritance from His hands if I will be sure to serve the Lord Christ at all times.

My prayer: Lord, I will serve you with all my heart and soul throughout this day. I am happy in your service. I will approach each task and responsibility with the intention of serving you. I ask only for your help as I serve you. Thank you for your promise of an inheritance. Thank you that I am your child and therefore your heir. What a marvelous inheritance is mine.

Today's Scriptures: Eph. 1:11; Eph. 1:14; 1 Pet. 1:4.

February 25

Today God says, *"Draw water from My wells of salvation."*

He promises me: "Behold, God is my salvation; I will trust, and not be afraid: for the Lord Jehovah is my strength and my song; he also is become my salvation. Therefore with joy shall ye draw water out of the wells of salvation. And in that day shall ye say, Praise the Lord" (Isa. 12:2-4).

My response to the Word: God is my salvation. I will trust in Him for He is my strength and my song. He invites me to draw water from His wells of salvation, and I do so with exceeding joy. His water of life refreshes me, cleanses me, and renews me. His great salvation supplies all my needs in every way. Praise the Lord!

My prayer: God, thank you for being my salvation. Thank you for giving me the water of life. I trust you, and as I do so, your perfect love takes away all fear. Praise your holy name!

Today's Scriptures: John 4:13-14; John 7:38; 1 John 4:18; Rev. 22:1.

February 26

Today God says, *"It is My good pleasure to give you the Kingdom."*

He promises me: "Fear not, little flock; for it is your Father's good pleasure to give you the kingdom" (Luke 12:32).

My response to the Word: The Kingdom of God exists wherever God rules and reigns. I am a part of His kingdom because He is my Lord. I have been born into His kingdom by His Spirit through the new birth. Paul wrote that God has, "delivered us from the power of darkness, and hath translated us into the Kingdom of his dear Son."

My prayer: Lord, thank you for delivering me out of the power of darkness and bringing me into your Kingdom where I now partake of the inheritance of the saints in light.

Today's Scriptures: John 3:5-6; Col. 1:12-13; 1 Thess. 2:12.

February 27

Today God says, *"You will do great things; you will prevail."*

He promises me: "Then Saul said to David, Blessed be thou, my son David: thou shalt both do great things, and also shalt still prevail" (1 Sam. 26:25).

My response to the Word: Though this promise was delivered to David by Saul, I know it applies to me also, because so many places in the Word declare that I will be an overcomer in life. I claim those promises for myself this day, because I know I am greatly blessed in every way. God gives me the strength to prevail in every situation.

My prayer: Father in heaven, thank you for the multitude of your promises which assure me that you will strengthen me in every situation. Because of your power I am a winner! You always give me the victory through my Lord Jesus Christ. I love you, Lord.

Today's Scriptures: John 14:12; Rom. 8:37; 1 Cor. 15:57; 1 John 5:4.

February 28

Today God says, *"I am the living God."*

He promises me: "As the Lord liveth, even what my God saith, that will I speak" (2 Chron. 18:13).

My response to the Word: I serve a living God. The empty tomb is proof that Jesus is alive. His Word is a living Word, and I will speak His Word to myself, to those around me, and to every situation that comes my way. "The word is nigh thee, even in thy mouth, and in thy heart: that is, the word of faith, which we preach."

My prayer: Father, you are the living God, I know that you are always at work in my life. I will hide your Word in my heart, and I will speak it forth at every opportunity. I will meditate in your Word for it is quick, it is alive, and it is powerful. Thank you for all the precious promises of your Word.

Today's Scriptures: Ps. 119:11; John 6:69; Rom. 10:8; Heb. 4:12.

February 29

Today God says, *"Nothing will ever separate you from my love."*

He promises me: "For I am persuaded, that neither death, nor life, nor angels, nor principalities, nor powers, nor things present, nor things to come, Nor height, nor depth, nor any other creature, shall be able to separate us from the love of God, which is in Christ Jesus our Lord" (Rom. 8:38-39).

My response to the Word: Nothing in the past, present, or future can separate me from the wonderful love of God which I found through Christ Jesus. His love is shed abroad in my heart by the Holy Spirit. God's love is a fabric that never fades, no matter how often it is washed in the waters of adversity and grief. I will walk in the sunshine of God's love throughout this day.

My prayer: Heavenly Father, I thank you for your everlasting love. It is stronger than any foe. It is the most excellent way of life. I cherish your love, and I love you with all my heart.

Today's Scriptures: Rom. 5:5; Rom. 5:8; 1 Cor. 12:31; 1 Cor. 13.

March 1

Today God says, *"Love never fails."*

He promises me: "Charity [love] never faileth: but whether there be prophecies, they shall fail; whether there be tongues, they shall cease; whether there be knowledge, it shall vanish away. For we know in part, and we prophesy in part. But when that which is perfect is come, then that which is in part shall be done away" (1 Cor. 13: 8-10).

My response to the Word: I love 1 Corinthians 13 — the love chapter, because it reminds me of the supremacy of love in all my relationships. First of all, in my relationship with God. I am able

to love only because He first loved me. Then, my
relationships with others. I will walk in God's
Spirit today because I know, ". . . the fruit of the
Spirit is love . . ."

My prayer: Lord, I love you because you first
loved me. I know that your love will never fail. I
will walk in your love throughout this day.
Thank you for loving me.

Today's Scriptures: 1 Cor. 13; Gal. 5:22; Eph.
5:2; 1 John 4:19.

March 2

Today God says, *"Perfect love casts out all fear."*

He promises me: "There is no fear in love;
but perfect love casteth out fear: because fear
hath torment. He that feareth is not made perfect
in love. We love him, because he first loved us"
(1 John 4:18-19).

My response to the Word: God's love is the
perfect antidote for fear. The comfort and security
of His love casts all fear out of my life. I have
known the torment of fear, but now I know the
sweet peace of God's love. I will fear neither
this day nor tomorrow, because I know God is
already there. In fact, He goes ahead of me, and
His spectacular love covers me.

My prayer: Lord God, I receive the fullness
of your perfect love which cast all the fears out of

my life. I will walk in your love, knowing that I will never have to fear again. You are my great God and Savior, and I praise your holy name!

Today's Scriptures: Ps. 36:7; 2 Cor. 13:11; 1 John 4:10.

March 3

Today God says, *"You are My friend."*

He promises me: "You are my friends, if you do whatsoever I command you. Henceforth I call you not servants; for the servant knoweth not what his lord doeth: but I have called you friends; for all things that I have heard of my Father I have made known unto you" (John 15:14-15).

My response to the Word: Like Abraham, I want to be the friend of God. God sees me as His friend when I obey the commandments of His Word. With His help, I will walk in obedience throughout this day, and I will meditate upon all the things God has taught me in His sacred Word. He is a true friend to me, One who "sticketh closer than a brother."

My prayer: Heavenly Father, friendship with you is more important to me than anything in this world. I will be your friend at all times. Thank you for sharing your Word with me.

Today's Scriptures: Prov. 18:24; Gal. 5:22-23; James 2:23.

March 4

Today God says, "*I have chosen you.*"

He promises me: "You have not chosen me, but I have chosen you, and ordained you, that ye should go and bring forth fruit, and that your fruit should remain: that whatsoever you shall ask of the Father in my name, he may give it you" (John 15:16).

My response to the Word: I realize that I cannot take credit for choosing God. He chose me. He chose me and ordained me to become a fruitful Christian. His amazing grace saved me from my sins, and gave my life a totally new direction and purpose. I will bear His fruit today as I walk in the Spirit. The fruit of the Spirit is ". . . love, joy, peace, longsuffering, gentleness, goodness, faith, Meekness, temperance: against such there is no law."

My prayer: Loving Lord, thank you for choosing me and equipping me to bear fruit for you. With your help, through the indwelling Spirit, I will be fruitful in every thing I do this day. I will walk in the knowledge that you have chosen me for your important purposes.

Today's Scriptures: Rom. 8:29-30; Eph. 1:11; Gal. 5:22-23.

March 5

Today God says, *"My mercy endures forever."*

He promises me: "O give thanks unto the Lord; for he is good: because his mercy endureth for ever" (Ps. 118:1).

My response to the Word: Yes, God is good. He is so good to me. He saves me, loves me, heals me, and helps me. I am exceedingly thankful to Him, and I know His mercy in my life will endure forever. What a wonderful promise this is! His goodness and His mercy will follow me all the days of my life, and I will dwell in His house forever!

My prayer: Dear Lord, thank you for your mercies in my life. I present my body, soul, and spirit as living sacrifices to you because I know this is my reasonable service of worship to you in light of all your mercies to me.

Today's Scriptures: Ps. 23:6; Ps. 70:5; Rom. 12:1; 2 Cor. 1:3.

March 6

Today God says, *"I am on your side."*

He promises me: "The Lord is on my side; I will not fear: what can man do unto me?" (Ps. 118:6).

My response to the Word: "What shall we then say to these things? If God be for us, who can be against us?" God is for me; He is on my side. Therefore, I will not fear anything or anyone. "The Lord is my light and my salvation; whom shall I fear? the Lord is the strength of my life; of whom shall I be afraid?"

My prayer: Dear God in heaven, I know you are on my side. I will set you always before me. I know you are at my right hand; therefore, I shall not be moved. Thank you, Father, for being on my side.

Today's Scriptures: Ps. 27:1; Rom. 8:31; Heb. 13:5.

March 7

Today God says, *"Christ lives in you."*

He promises me: "I am crucified with Christ: nevertheless I live; yet not I, but Christ liveth in me: and the life I now live in the flesh I live by the faith of the Son of God, who loved me, and gave himself for me" (Gal. 2:20).

My response to the Word: Christ, the Anointed One, lives in me. His name is called Wonderful, Counselor, the mighty God, the everlasting Father, and the Prince of Peace. He is the way, the truth, and the life. He is everything to me. He created all things, and by Him all things consist. Truly Christ in me is my hope of glory.

My prayer: Dear Lord, you have given so much to me. I thank you for life itself — for the abundant life you have imparted to me through Jesus Christ.

Today's Scriptures: Isa. 9:6; John 14:6; Col. 1:16-17, 27; Col. 3:11.

March 8

Today God says, *"My Word is a light unto your path."*

He promises me: "Thy word is a lamp unto my feet, and a light unto my path" (Ps. 119:105).

My response to the Word: God's Word is a lamp unto my feet and a light unto my path. I will walk in the light it provides throughout this day. The light of God's Word fills me with faith, dispells the darkness, reveals the pitfalls, frightens the creatures of darkness, and directs my steps. I will remember that Paul calls the Bible, "the sword of the Spirit," and I know that the sword of the Spirit never grows dull with use. Instead, it keeps getting brighter and sharper.

My prayer: Heavenly Father, thank you for the light of your Word which clearly shows me which steps to take as I proceed through life. I will walk in the light of your Word today.

Today's Scriptures: Eph. 6:17; James 1:22; 1 John 2:14.

March 9

Today God says, *"My Word will keep you from sin."*

He promises me: "Thy word have I hid in mine heart, that I might not sin against thee" (Ps. 119:11).

My response to the Word: I love the Word of God. It is powerful and it is alive. It protects me and it defends me. When I wonder, as the Psalmist did, how I can cleanse my way, I am reminded of the truths of the Bible. I will take heed to the Word of God throughout this day. I will treasure the Word in my heart, and as Jesus did in the wilderness, I will defeat the enemy by quoting the powerful truths of God's Word.

My prayer: Almighty God, thank you for your Word which keeps me from sin by strengthening me and showing me how to live a righteous life before you. I love your Word, and I will hide it in my heart so that I will avoid all sin.

Today's Scriptures: Ps. 119:9; Luke 4; Heb. 4:12.

March 10

Today God says, *"Draw near to Me, and I will draw near to you."*

He promises me: "Draw nigh to God, and he will draw nigh to you" (James 4:8).

My response to the Word: The Lord invites me to draw near to Him, and He promises me that if I will do this, He will draw near to me. First, however, I must remember to do the following: "Submit yourselves therefore to God. Resist the devil, and he will flee from you" Therefore, throughout this day I will submit my entire life to my Father-God. I will resist the devil every time he tries to throw me off-track, and I will be sure to draw near to God each step of the way.

My prayer: Heavenly Father, thank you for all the promises of your Word, and for the invitations you extend to me so graciously. Thank you for inviting me to draw near to you, and for your promise that you will respond by drawing near to me. I draw near to you, Father, and I will walk in your presence throughout this day.

Today's Scriptures: John 15:1-7; John 15:10; James 4:7; 1 John 2:28.

March 11

Today God says, "*I will preserve you from all evil.*"

He promises me, "The Lord shall preserve thee from all evil: he shall preserve thy soul. The Lord shall preserve thy going out and thy coming in from this time forth, and even for evermore" (Ps. 121:7-8).

My response to the Word: I receive and believe God's promises of preservation. He will preserve me from all evil throughout this day. He will preserve my coming and going throughout this day as well. Indeed, He will preserve me forevermore. Today, whenever I am presented with the choice between two evils, I will choose neither; when presented with the choice between two goods, I will choose both.

My prayer: God, my Father in heaven, thank you for your protective love in my life. I know that I have no reason to fear evil any longer because you have promised to preserve me from all evil. I claim your promise for this day.

Today's Scriptures: Luke 11:4; Gal. 1:4; Eph. 6:13.

March 12

Today God says, *"Come unto Me, and I will give you rest."*

He promises me: "Come unto me, all ye that labour and are heavy laden, and I will give you rest. Take my yoke upon you, and learn of me; for I am meek and lowly in heart: and ye shall find rest unto your souls. For my yoke is easy, and my burden is light" (Matt. 11:28-30).

My response to the Word: God's gracious invitation, extended by Jesus Christ, is simply for me to come to Him. If I will choose to do this, He

promises to give me rest from all my burdens.
He wants me to share His yoke because His yoke
is easy, and His burden is light. I will obey this
commandment at all times today, especially when
I am feeling weary, burdened, and tired. Jesus is
the answer to my every need!

My prayer: Lord, I come to you just as I am.
I lay my burdens at the foot of the cross. I know
that you are the great Burden-bearer, and you will
sustain me. I experience your blessed rest even as
I am praying. Thank you, Father.

Today's Scriptures: Ps. 37:7; Heb. 4:1; Heb. 4:9.

March 13

Today God says, *"Prove Me with your tithes and
offerings."*

He promises me: "Bring ye all the tithes into
the storehouse, that there may be meat in mine
house, and prove me now herewith, saith the Lord
of hosts, if I will not open you the windows of
heaven, and pour you out a blessing, that there
shall not be room enough to receive it" (Mal. 3:10).

My response to the Word: God asks me to prove
Him with my tithes and offerings. He promises to
bless me abundantly if I do. I realize that all I am
and all I have is His to begin with; therefore, I
will return the first-fruits of my income to Him. I
will obey the words of Jesus who said, "Lay not

up for yourselves treasures upon earth, where moth and rust doth corrupt, and where thieves break through and steal: But lay up for yourselves treasures in heaven."

My prayer: Heavenly Father, thank you for all that you have given to me. I am the steward over your property; therefore, I will give back to you through my tithes and offerings.

Today's Scriptures: Matt. 6:19-20; Matt. 10:8; 2 Cor. 9:7.

March 14

Today God says, *"I will pour out an abundant blessing upon you and yours."*

He promises me: "Prove me now herewith, saith the Lord of hosts, if I will not open you the windows of heaven, and pour you out a blessing, that there shall not be room enough to receive it. And I will rebuke the devourer for your sakes, and he shall not destroy the fruits of your ground" (Mal. 3:10-11).

My response to the Word: God wants me to tithe my income and give offerings to Him. This I will do faithfully. He promises me that He will pour out a blessing upon me that will be so great that I will not have room enough to receive it. He also promises to rebuke the devourer for my sake. I rejoice in the certain knowledge that His blessings are being poured out of the very windows of heaven, and Satan no longer has a right to bring destruction to me or mine.

My prayer: Loving Lord, I have freely received so much from your hands. I commit to you that I will return my tithes to you and give freely at every opportunity. Thank you for your blessings in my life.

Today's Scriptures: Deut. 28:2; Prov. 10:6; Eph. 1:3.

March 15

Today God says, *"No weapon formed against you shall prosper."*

He promises me: "No weapon that is formed against thee shall prosper; and every tongue that shall rise against thee in judgment thou shalt condemn. This is the heritage of the servants of the Lord, and their righteousness is of me, saith the Lord" (Isa. 54:17).

My response to the Word: God is my sure defense. He is protecting me from all evil. I know that no weapon that is formed against me shall prosper. Every tongue that rises against me in judgment will be condemned by my Father in heaven. This is my inheritance as a servant of the Lord. He has imparted His righteousness to me. Praise His holy name!

My prayer: Heavenly Father, thank you for assuring me over and over again in your Word that you will protect me from the evil one, from evil people, and from evil in every form. I receive your promise, believe it, and I walk in complete confidence in you.

Today's Scriptures: Ps. 18:3; Ps. 59:1; Ps. 143:9.

March 16

Today God says, *"I will not permit you to be tempted beyond your ability to endure."*

He promises me: "There hath no temptation taken you but such as is common to man: but God is faithful, who will not suffer you to be tempted above that ye are able; but will with the temptation also make a way to escape, that ye may be able to bear it" (1 Cor. 10:13).

My response to the Word: When temptations come my way, my faithful Lord will be there to help see me through. He will not permit me to be tempted beyond my ability to endure. He will show me the way out of every temptation. Throughout this day I will be vigilant, and I will remember that temptation is not sin, but playing with temptation will lead me into sin. Therefore, I will resist all temptation with the power of the Word, the blood of Jesus, and the Holy Spirit.

My prayer: Lord, I thank you for your promise that you will not permit me to be tempted beyond my ability to endure. Through your power I will resist all temptations that come to me this day.

Today's Scriptures: Rom. 8:13; James 1:2; 1 Pet. 1:6-7; 2 Pet. 2:9.

March 17

Today God says, *"At My right hand there are pleasures forevermore."*

He promises me: "Thou wilt shew me the path of life: in thy presence is fulness of joy; at thy right hand there are pleasures for evermore" (Ps. 16:11).

My response to the Word: How I delight in the presence of God. As I experience His presence through worship and the Word I am filled with joy. How wonderful it is to know that there will be eternal pleasures at His right hand. The place to be happy is here, the time to be happy is now, the way to be happy is to love God and others. I will walk in God's joy and happiness throughout this day as I practice His wonderful presence.

My prayer: Thank you, Father, for giving me joy. I believe your promise that I will have pleasures forevermore in your presence. I will let your joy, happiness, and pleasures fill the pathway of my life.

Today's Scriptures: Ps. 36:8; Isa. 61:10; 1 Pet. 1:8.

March 18

Today God says, *"Wear the protective armor I've given to you."*

He promises me: "Put on the whole armour of God, that ye may be able to stand against the wiles of the devil" (Eph. 6:11).

My response to the Word: I will put on every piece of God's armor, and I will wear it throughout this day. I will gird my loins with truth. The breastplate of righteousness will protect my chest and heart. On my feet I will wear the preparation of the gospel of peace. I will use the shield of faith to quench all the fiery darts of the wicked one. I will protect my head and mind with the helmet of salvation, and I will wage my warfare with the sword of the Spirit (the Word of God). I will put on each piece of God's armor carefully, praying always with all prayer and supplication in the Spirit. God will protect me.

My prayer: Lord God, thank you for the armor you've given to me to protect me from all evil. I will wear it confidently throughout this day.

Today's Scriptures: Ps. 84:11; 2 Cor. 6:7; Eph. 6:10-18.

March 19

Today God says, *"Faith is the victory that overcomes the world."*

He promises me: "For whatsoever is born of God overcometh the world: and this is the victory that overcometh the world, even our faith" (1 John 5:4).

My response to the Word: Faith is a gift God has bestowed upon me as a part of my birthright as His child. Faith comes as I hear His Word and meditate on it. He has promised me that I will overcome the world as I walk in faith. Therefore, I choose to walk in faith throughout this day. Faith will help me to walk fearlessly, run confidently, and live victoriously throughout this day.

My prayer: Father, my faith is in you and your wonderful Word. I believe your Word. It renews my mind and fills me with faith. I claim your promise for today: that I will overcome the world. Thank you, Father.

Today's Scriptures: Rom. 10:17; Col. 1:23; 1 Tim. 6:11-12; Heb. 6:12.

March 20

Today God says, *"I know My sheep, and My sheep know Me."*

He promises me: "I am the good shepherd, and know my sheep, and are known of mine" (John 10:14).

My response to the Word: Jesus, the Good Shepherd, knows me personally. He knows my name, and He knows everything about me. He said, "As the Father knoweth me, even so know I the Father: and I lay down my life for the sheep." This causes me to proclaim, "The Lord is my shepherd," and to know that He loves me and will meet all my needs. He laid down His life for me. I will spend time today getting to know my Shepherd better.

My prayer: Lord, you are my Shepherd. I shall not want. You make me to lie down in green pastures. You lead me beside the still waters. You restore my soul. You love me and I love you. Thank you, Father.

Today's Scriptures: Ps. 23:1; John 10:11; Heb. 13:20.

March 21

Today God says, *"Heaven is your home."*

He promises me: "Let not your heart be troubled: ye believe in God, believe also in me. In my Father's house are many mansions: if it were not so, I would have told you. I go to prepare a place for you. And if I go and prepare a place for you, I will come again, and receive you unto myself; that where I am, there ye may be also" (John 14:1-3).

My response to the Word: There is a lot of truth to the song that says, "This world is not my home; I'm just a-passin' through. My treasures are laid up somewhere beyond the blue. The angels beckon me from heaven's open door, and I can't feel at home in this world anymore." Heaven is my future home. I look forward with joy to the time when I will be able to join the heavenly host before Gods throne, in saying, "Holy, holy, holy, Lord God Almighty, which was and is to come."

My prayer: Heavenly Father, thank you for my heavenly home, which Jesus has already prepared for me. I look forward to His return. In heaven, worshiping you will be my greatest joy, as it already is.

Today's Scriptures: Col. 1:5; 2 Tim. 4:18; Heb. 12:22; 1 Pet. 1:4; Rev. 4:8.

March 22

Today God says, *"My Spirit will guide you into all truth."*

He promises me: "Howbeit when he, the Spirit of truth, is come, he will guide you into all truth" (John 16:13).

My response to the Word: After Jesus ascended to heaven He sent the Holy Spirit to empower me, comfort me, and guide me into all truth. I trust Him to guide me throughout this day. It's such an adventure to be led by the Spirit of God. He opens door and windows into new dimensions of life. He reminds me of the truths of God's Word. Throughout this day I will let Him guide me, and I will remember, "And ye shall know the truth, and the truth shall make you free."

My prayer: Lord, your Word is truth, and your Spirit guides me into all truth. Jesus is the truth, and He has set me free. I will walk in the truth of your Word throughout this day.

Today's Scriptures: John 8:32; John 14:6; John 14:17; 1 John 5:6.

March 23

Today God says, *"I will make your way prosperous."*

He promises me: "This book of the law shall not depart out of thy mouth; but thou shalt meditate therein day and night, that thou mayest observe to do according to all that is written therein: for then thou shalt make thy way prosperous, and then thou shalt have good success" (Josh. 1:8).

My response to the Word: The Word of God contains vital truths for my daily life. I will meditate upon the Scriptures throughout this day, and I will apply them to my life through faith and obedience. This will ensure that I will know prosperity, and it will grant me success. God tells me, "Have I not commanded thee? Be

strong and of a good courage; be not afraid,
neither be thou dismayed: for the Lord thy God
is with thee whithersoever thou goest."

My prayer: Lord God, I know you are with
me each step of my way. I will walk in obedience
to your Word today, and I know you will grant
me prosperity, success, courage, and peace. Thank
you, Father.

Today's Scriptures: Josh. 1:9; Ps. 35:27; Isa. 48:15.

March 24

Today God says, *"I will give you good success."*

He promises me: "This book of the law shall
not depart out of thy mouth; but thou shalt meditate
therein day and night, that thou mayest observe to
do according to all that is written therein: for then
thou shalt make thy way prosperous, and then
thou shalt have good success" (Josh. 1:8).

My response to the Word: The book of the
Law, for believers today, is the Bible — the most
precious book of all. I will meditate upon God's
Word throughout this day, because this is the key
to learning God's will and it is the key to walking
in obedience to the Word. God promises me,
that if I will do these things, He will make my
way prosperous and He will give me good
success. My Father in heaven wants me to be
successful at all times!

My prayer: Heavenly Father, thank you for your Word which is filled with so many promises of good things from your hands. I believe your Word and I claim your promise that you will give me good success.

Today's Scriptures: Ps. 1:3; Ps. 122:6; 3 John 2.

March 25

Today God says, *"Nothing is too hard for Me."*

He promises me: "Is any thing too hard for the Lord?" (Gen. 18:14).

My response to the Word: This verse is set in the context of the Lord promising Isaac to Abraham and Sarah. Sarah responded by laughing and saying, "Shall I of a surety bear a child, which am old?" She had doubt concerning God's word to her. The Lord responded to her question with a rhetorical question (one which does not require an answer): "Is any thing too hard for the Lord?" I know the answer — nothing, absolutely nothing — is too hard for my God.

My prayer: Almighty God, you are able to do anything. I will never doubt your Word, because I know you are "able to do exceeding abundantly above all that we ask or think, according to the power that worketh in us."

Today's Scriptures: Gen. 18:14; 2 Cor. 9:8; Eph. 3:20; Jude 24.

March 26

Today God says, *"I am your Creator."*

He promises me: "For by him were all things created, that are in heaven, and that are in earth, visible and invisible, whether they be thrones, or dominions, or principalities, or powers: all things were created by him, and for him" (Col. 1:16).

My response to the Word: I believe that God is the Creator of the entire universe, and that includes *me.* He created me for His pleasure. The Word proclaims, "Thou art worthy, O Lord, to receive glory and honour and power: for thou hast created all things, and for thy pleasure they are and were created." I was created for the Father's pleasure, and throughout this day I want to please Him.

My prayer: Thank you, Father, for creating me to have fellowship with you. I want my life to give you pleasure at all times. You are worthy of all my devotion, praise, and service. I give myself to you.

Today's Scriptures: Gen. 1; Rom. 1:20; Rev. 4:11.

March 27

Today God says, *"I am the Potter; you are the clay."*

He promises me: "But now, O Lord, thou art our father; we are the clay, and thou our potter; and we all are the work of thy hand" (Isa. 64:8).

My response to the Word: God is my Father, and He is the Potter who is shaping my life. He is changing me from glory to glory. He is conforming me to the image of His Son, my Lord and Savior, Jesus Christ. He is not finished with me. My loving heavenly Father is at work in my life. He will continue His workmanship as long as I live.

My prayer: Heavenly Father, you are the Potter; I am the clay. Have your own way in my life throughout this day. Mold me, shape me, use me, I pray. Thank you, Lord, for your continual workmanship in my life.

Today's Scriptures: Rom. 8:29; 1 Cor. 15:51-52; 2 Cor. 3:18.

March 28

Today God says, *"I am the Lord who heals you."*

He promises me: "And said, If thou wilt diligently hearken to the voice of the Lord thy God, and wilt do that which is right in his sight, and wilt give ear to his commandments, and keep all his statutes, I will put none of these diseases upon thee, which I have brought upon the Egyptians: for I am the Lord that healeth thee" (Exod. 15:26).

My response to the Word: Throughout this day I will diligently hearken to the voice of my Lord. I will do what is right in His eyes. I will obey His commandments. I will believe His Word. He promises me that He will keep me from disease, and bring healing to me. I believe this promise of His Word, and I claim it for my life and for the lives of my loved ones. God is the Lord that heals — His healing power is at work in my life even now.

My prayer: Lord God, thank you for showing me the way to health and healing through your Word. If I will keep your Word, you will protect me from disease. If I will walk in your precepts, you will heal me. Throughout this day I will keep your Word and I will walk in its healing light.

Today's Scriptures: Mal. 4:2; Matt. 4:23; Matt. 9:35.

March 29

Today God says, *"I am the Great Physician."*

He promises me: "But unto you that fear my name shall the Sun of righteousness arise with healing in his wings; and ye shall go forth, and grow up as calves of the stall. And ye shall tread down the wicked; for they shall be ashes under the soles of your feet in the day that I shall do this, saith the Lord of hosts" (Mal. 4:2).

My response to the Word: The Sun of righteousness is the Lord Jesus Christ, the Great Physician of my soul and body. When He arises in my life, healing comes to me. I will let Him arise throughout this day. Medical doctors sometimes measure physical health by the way the tongue looks; the Great Physician measures spiritual health by how the tongue speaks. I will thank God for providing health and healing for myself and others throughout this day.

My prayer: Thank you, Lord, for the promises of your Word which declare that I can walk in good health throughout my life. Fill me with your Spirit, I ask, because I know this truth: "If the Spirit of him that raised up Jesus from the dead dwell in you, he that raised up Christ from the dead shall also quicken your mortal bodies by his Spirit that dwelleth in you."

Today's Scriptures: Exod. 15:26; Ps. 103:3; Luke 9:6; Rom. 8:11.

March 30

Today God says, "*A merry heart will do you good.*"

He promises me: "A merry heart doeth good like a medicine: but a broken spirit drieth the bones" (Prov. 17:22).

My response to the Word: I will try to maintain a cheerful and joyful disposition throughout this day because I know God's Word is true. A merry heart does me good like a medicine. I will remember that true happiness is not based on what I have in my hands, but it is something I carry in my heart. Happiness consists of a healthy mental attitude, a grateful spirit, a clear conscience, and a heart full of God's life. I purpose to hold onto each of these throughout this day.

My prayer: God, thank you for the joy and happiness that come from knowing you. I will foster these qualities today, knowing that keeping my heart merry will do me good like a medicine.

Today's Scriptures: Neh. 8:10; Rom. 5:11; Col. 1:11.

March 31

Today God says, *"You are fearfully and wonderfully made."*

He promises me: "I will praise thee; for I am fearfully and wonderfully made: marvellous are thy works; and that my soul knoweth right well. My substance was not hid from thee, when I was made in secret, and curiously wrought in the lowest parts of the earth" (Ps. 139:14-15).

My response to the Word: God created me for His specific purposes. I am fearfully and wonderfully made. This fact alone gives me healthy self-esteem. I am one of God's works, and His works are marvelous. I have been hand-crafted by the Almighty Ruler of the universe. His works are perfect, and He continues to shape and mold me after His will. Praise God!

My prayer: Almighty God, thank you for creating me for your special purposes, and for assuring me that I am one of your special creations. I will walk in the joy of this wonderful truth throughout this day.

Today's Scriptures: Gen. 1:27; Rom. 8:29; Eph. 2:10.

April 1

Today God says, *"My kingdom is an everlasting kingdom."*

He promises me: "Thy kingdom is an everlasting kingdom, and thy dominion endureth throughout all generations. The Lord upholdeth all that fall, and raiseth up all those that be bowed down" (Ps. 145:13-14).

My response to the Word: God is the King in charge of the only eternal kingdom. His dominion will never end. His kingdom knows no bounds.

He rules the universe, and His kingdom is above me, around me, and within me, because I am His subject. I will let Him rule and reign in my life today.

My prayer: Lord, you are the King of kings and the Lord of lords. I give you full control of my life this day.

Today's Scriptures: Luke 1:33; Rom. 14:17; Col. 1:13; 1 Thess. 2:12.

April 2

Today God says, *"Hearken unto Me and I will keep you safe from all evil."*

He promises me: "But whoso hearkeneth unto me shall dwell safely, and shall be quiet from fear of evil" (Prov. 1:33).

My response to the Word: Throughout this day I will listen for my Lord's voice, and I will take heed to His Word. I rejoice in His promise that He will keep me safe, and I will be quiet from all fear of evil. To hearken to the Lord is to listen to His Word and obey it. I will walk in obedience to the Lord throughout this day.

My prayer: Father, I love you, and I know you love me. Thank you for your promises of security and peace. I claim them as my own as I take the necessary steps of obedience today.

Today's Scriptures: Ps. 4:8; Prov. 21:31; Prov. 29:25.

April 3

Today God says, *"Obey my commandments, and live a long and productive life."*

He promises me: "My son, forget not my law; but let thine heart keep my commandments: for length of days, and long life, and peace, shall they add to thee" (Prov. 3:1-2).

My response to the Word: God's commands are contained in His Word. I will remember His Word throughout this day. I will keep His commandments in my heart and in my actions. He promises me that such obedience will give me a long life and peace. As I think about this promise, I realize that God puts forth His commands and principles for my good. These are not given to restrict my life, but to bless it. Therefore, I will walk in obedience to God's Word throughout this day.

My prayer: Heavenly Father, thank you for your Word. Thank you for giving me your commandments to protect me. With your help, I will obey your Word throughout this day.

Today's Scriptures: Acts 5:29; 2 Cor. 10:5; Eph. 6:2-3; Heb. 5:8.

April 4

Today God says, *"Acknowledge Me at all times, and I will direct you."*

He promises me: "Trust in the Lord with all thine heart; and lean not unto thine own understanding. In all thy ways acknowledge him, and he shall direct thy paths" (Prov. 3:5-6).

My response to the Word: I will trust in the Lord with all my heart. I will stop leaning upon my own understanding. In all my ways I will acknowledge the Lord, and I know He will direct my paths. To trust the Lord I must know Him, and I will avail myself of every opportunity to get to know Him better through prayer, His Word, worship, and praise. He is always only a prayer away.

My prayer: Lord, I trust you with all my heart. I will acknowledge you in everything I do this day. Thank you for your promise to direct me. I purpose now to obey and follow your direction.

Today's Scriptures: Ps. 25:9; Ps. 32:8; Isa. 58:11.

April 5

Today God says, *"Don't despise My correction in your life."*

He promises me: "My son, despise not the chastening of the Lord; neither be weary of his correction: For whom the Lord loveth he correcteth; even as a father the son in whom he delighteth" (Prov. 3:11-12).

My response to the Word: God loves me. He is my Father. When He corrects me or chastens me it is because He loves me. I know I need His correction in my life. Therefore, I will not resist it nor despise it when it comes because I know it will serve its intended purpose of teaching me and training me in righteousness. It is thrilling to know that the Lord takes delight in me.

My prayer: Lord God, thank you for the discipline you bring into my life to help me become the best I can be. I receive your loving chastening and correction because I know they are good for me.

Today's Scriptures: Job 5:17; Jer. 10:24; Heb. 12:8.

April 6

Today God says, *"My wisdom gives you happiness."*

He promises me: "Happy is the man that findeth wisdom, and the man that getteth understanding" (Prov. 3:13).

My response to the Word: God promises to give me His wisdom if I will seek it. His Word declares, "If any of you lack wisdom, let him ask of God, that giveth to all men liberally, and upbraideth not; and it shall be given him. But let him ask in faith, nothing wavering. For he that wavereth is like a wave of the sea driven with the wind and tossed." I will ask for God's wisdom throughout this day, and I know the end result will be happiness.

My prayer: All-wise heavenly Father, thank you for your promises of wisdom and happiness. Thank you for showing me that wisdom and happiness are inseparable, that I can't have one without the other. I will walk in your wisdom throughout this day.

Today's Scriptures: Ps. 111:10; Prov. 4:7; Acts 6:3; James 1:5-6.

April 7

Today God says, *"My words are life to you."*

He promises me: "My son, attend to my words; incline thine ear unto my sayings. Let them not depart from thine eyes; keep them in the midst of thine heart. For they are life unto those that find them, and health to all their flesh" (Prov. 4:20-22).

My response to the Word: I will obey the words of the Lord throughout this day because I know they will give me life and health. I will study the Word of the Lord, and always endeavor to walk in His paths. The Bible is a living book, and its words impart spiritual life and health to me. The Word of God contains the vitamins for a happy, healthy, and contented life.

My prayer: Thank you for your Word, heavenly Father. I will walk in its life, health, and strength throughout this day. Your words truly are life and health to me.

Today's Scriptures: 1 Tim. 4:5; Heb. 4:12; James 1:21.

April 8

Today God says, *"Keep your heart with all diligence."*

He promises me: "Keep thy heart with all diligence; for out of it are the issues of life" (Prov. 4:23).

My response to the Word: It is my responsibility to keep my heart pure. Jesus said, "Blessed are the pure in heart: for they shall see God." I want to see God — in my life in the here-and-now and throughout eternity. Someone once said, "When God measures a man, He puts the tape around his heart instead of his head." Therefore, I will endeavor to keep my heart with all diligence throughout this day.

My prayer: Father, thank you for your Word. Help me to keep my heart with all diligence throughout this day. I realize that the issues of my life stem from the attitudes of my heart.

Today's Scriptures: Ps. 51:10; Ps. 57:7; Ps. 108:1; Matt. 5:8; Heb. 4:12.

April 9

Today God says, *"You belong to Christ."*

He promises me: "Whether Paul, or Apollos, or Cephas, or the world, or life, or death, or things present, or things to come, all are yours; And ye are Christ's; and Christ is God's" (1 Cor. 3:22-23).

My response to the Word: God blesses me with so much. The greatest blessing of all, however, is that I belong to Christ. He redeemed me with His blood. He loved me so much that He laid down His life for me. Throughout this day, I will remember these important words: "What? know ye not that your body is the temple of the Holy Ghost which is in you, which ye have of God, and ye are not your own? For ye are bought with a price: therefore glorify God in your body, and in your spirit, which are God's."

My prayer: Dear Lord, I believe that Jesus Christ died for me, and I have trusted in Him for my salvation. Now I belong to Him, and I love Him with all my heart. Thank you for sending your Son to die for me.

Today's Scriptures: Rom. 12:1-2; 1 Cor. 6:19-20; 1 Cor. 7:23.

April 10

Today God says, *"You are justified in the name of the Lord Jesus."*

He promises me: "And such were some of you: but ye are washed, but ye are sanctified, but ye are justified in the name of the Lord Jesus, and by the Spirit of our God" (1 Cor. 6:11).

My response to the Word: The word "justified" literally means "just as if I'd never sinned." This is amazing news to me. Even though I was a sinner, I've now been justified, and God, my heavenly Father, sees me as His perfected child. In the name of the Lord Jesus Christ I've been washed, sanctified, and justified. Praise the name of Jesus!

My prayer: Heavenly Father, thank you for justifying me in the name of the Lord Jesus, by your Spirit. Indeed, I know you have set me free from the law of sin and death.

Today's Scriptures: Rom. 4:25; Rom. 5:1; Rom. 8:30.

April 11

Today God says, *"I am not the author of confusion."*

He promises me: "For God is not the author of confusion, but of peace, as in all churches of the saints" (1 Cor. 14:33).

My response to the Word: Whenever I experience confusion I lose the peace of God. God always gives me clarity of thought and purpose; He never confuses me. Life, after all, is simple when we follow God's ways; it is usually we ourselves who create or permit the circumstances that create confusion. Jesus said, "Peace I leave with you, my peace I give unto you." I will walk in the peace Jesus gives to me throughout this day. I will renew my mind with God's Word.

My prayer: Father, help me to remember that when confusion comes I need to get alone with you and your Word. Being in your presence gives me such peace that all confusion is eradicated. Your Word brings light and direction to me. Thank you, Lord.

Today's Scriptures: Ps. 119:130; John 14:27; 1 Cor. 7:15; Gal. 5:22-23.

April 12

Today God says, *"Whatever you ask Me for, in the name of Jesus, I will give to you."*

He promises me: "Verily, verily, I say unto you, Whatsoever ye shall ask the Father in my name, he will give it you" (John 16:23).

My response to the Word: God, my heavenly Father, never tires of hearing me pray. In fact, He wants me to pray at all times. He has established prayer as the avenue of fellowship and blessing. In fact, praying in the name of Jesus along with faith-filled receiving will give me fullness of joy. Jesus said, "Hitherto have ye asked nothing in my name: ask, and ye shall receive, that your joy may be full." I will pray in the name of Jesus throughout this day.

My prayer: Father, In the name of Jesus, through faith in your Word, I ask for the following:

_____

_____. I receive now by faith. I know you hear me, and I know you will answer me. Thank you, Father, for the fullness of joy this gives to me.

Today's Scriptures: Mark 11:22, 24; John 16:24; John 16:26; Phil. 2:9.

April 13

Today God says, "*I have overcome the world.*"

He promises me: "These things I have spoken unto you, that in me ye might have peace. In the world ye shall have tribulation: but be of good cheer; I have overcome the world" (John 16:33).

My response to the Word: God loves me, and He wants me to experience the peace that comes from knowing that Jesus has already overcome the world. He also wants me to know that it is through faith in Him that I too have victory over the world. This enables me to be cheerful throughout the day. The Prince of peace has already defeated the evil and sin of the world. I will remember that the world at its worst needs me to be at my best. My best is only achieved as I yield my life to Jesus Christ, my Lord and Savior.

My prayer: Lord, I yield my life to you. You have given me victory over the world. Even when worldly tribulations come to me, I take heart in the fact that Jesus has already overcome the world. This assurance gives me great peace. Thank you, Lord.

Today's Scriptures: 1 John 5:4-5; Rev. 1:8; Rev. 2:7.

April 14

Today God says, *"You are My righteousness in Christ."*

He promises me: "For he hath made him to be sin for us, who knew no sin; that we might be made the righteousness of God in him" (2 Cor. 5:21).

My response to the Word: It is simply amazing to reflect on the realization that Jesus Christ, the spotless Lamb of God, became sin for me so that God's righteousness could be imparted to me. I know I haven't lost the ability to sin, but I have certainly lost the desire to sin, and this is because of what Jesus did for me. Jesus became sin for me so that I could become the righteousness of God in Him.

My prayer: Father, thank you for the liberating truths of your Word. Thank you for sending Jesus to become sin for me so that your righteousness could be manifested in my life. I will walk in your righteousness throughout this day.

Today's Scriptures: Gal. 5:5; Phil. 3:9; 2 Pet. 1:1.

April 15

Today God says, *"Jesus became poor so that you could become rich."*

He promises me: "For ye know the grace of our Lord Jesus Christ, that, though he was rich, yet for your sakes he became poor, that ye through his poverty might be rich" (2 Cor. 8:9).

My response to the Word: God's grace is so wonderful. He sent His only begotten Son, my Lord and Savior Jesus Christ, from the riches of heaven to the poverty of the human condition so that I could be enriched through faith in Him. Even though I may or may not be rich in the things of this world, I possess the unsearchable riches of Christ.

My prayer: Heavenly Father, thank you for blessing me with so many riches. The greatest treasure of all is to know Jesus Christ. He has truly made me rich, and I will remember the riches He has blessed me with throughout this day.

Today's Scriptures: Eph. 1:11; Eph. 1:18; Eph. 3:8; Eph. 3:16.

April 16

Today God says, *"The sorrow I impart to you leads you to repentance."*

He promises me: "For godly sorrow worketh repentance to salvation not to be repented of: but the sorrow of the world worketh death" (2 Cor. 7:10).

My response to the Word: I can't even boast about my repentance for my sins. Such repentance is a gift of God's grace to me. His sorrow works repentance into my soul, giving me spiritual life. This is unlike the sorrow of the world which leads to death. I realize that true repentance has at least two aspects: it looks upon past failures and sins with a weeping eye, and it looks upon the future with a watchful eye. I will be vigilant in my stance against sin throughout this day.

My prayer: Heavenly Father, thank you for your goodness which leads me to repentance. When I confess my sins, you are faithful and just to forgive my sins and to cleanse me from all unrighteousness. I confess my sins to you now and receive your forgiveness and cleansing. Thank you, Father.

Today's Scriptures: Rom. 2:4; 2 Cor. 7:9; 2 Tim. 2:25; 1 John 1:9.

April 17

Today God says, *"You are a new creation."*

He promises me: "Therefore if any man be in Christ, he is a new creature: old things are passed away; behold, all things are become new" (2 Cor. 5:17).

My response to the Word: I am a new creation in Christ Jesus. I am born again by God's Spirit. Gone is the guilt of the past, and gone is the fear of the future. Truly, all things have become new in my life. Throughout this day, I will meditate upon the Word of God because I know that the knowledge, understanding, and appropriation of God's Word are the means by which I grow spiritually. I will walk in newness of life today.

My prayer: Father God, thank you for making me a new creation in Christ, my Lord. You have transformed me from the old ways of life into an entirely new creation. I am your child. It is exciting to walk with you.

Today's Scriptures: John 3:1-6; Rom. 6:4; Eph. 4:24; 1 Pet. 1:23; 1 Pet. 2:2.

April 18

Today God says, *"Your effectual, fervent prayer will avail much."*

He promises me: "Confess your faults one to another, and pray one for another, that ye may be healed. The effectual fervent prayer of a righteous man availeth much" (James 5:16).

My response to the Word: The power of prayer goes beyond my ability to understand. In spite of this, I know that God wants me to pray, and He promises to hear and answer my prayers when I pray according to His will. Throughout this day I will remember that God, my heavenly Father, is only a prayer away. I will claim His promise, "Call unto me, and I will answer thee, and shew thee great and mighty things, which thou knowest not."

My prayer: Lord, I believe in you and I believe your Word. Thank you for the access you give to me through prayer and that my prayers are powerful and effective. I will pray without ceasing today.

Today's Scriptures: Jer. 33:3; 1 Thess. 5:17; 1 John 5:14-15.

April 19

Today God says, *"To live is Christ, and to die is gain."*

He promises me: "For to me to live is Christ, and to die is gain" (Phil. 1:21).

My response to the Word: Christ is the center of my life. I live for Him. He is my Lord and Savior. When I die, I will continue to be with Him in a far-better realm than this earth. Heaven is far better than this present world, praise God! Throughout this day I will let my mind be a mind through which Christ thinks His thoughts, my heart will be the heart through which He loves, my voice a voice through which He speaks, and my hand a hand through which He helps others.

My prayer: Lord, I thank you for Christ who truly is the center of my life. Throughout this day I will let my life, my words, my thoughts, and my actions be Christ-centered. Thank you for your help in my daily life.

Today's Scriptures: Col. 3:3-4; 2 Tim. 1:1; 1 John 5:11.

April 20

Today God says, *"Rejoice always."*

He promises me: Rejoice in the Lord alway: and again I say, Rejoice. Let your moderation be known unto all men. The Lord is at hand" (Phil. 4:4-5).

My response to the Word: God is at hand, and this fact alone causes me to rejoice at all times. My rejoicing comes from the realization that God is my Father who is always with me. Throughout this day I will keep my heart from hatred and my mind from worry. I will live simply and fill my heart with love. Rejoicing in the Lord and praising Him will help me to keep my perspective at all times.

My prayer: Lord, I will spend this day rejoicing as I contemplate all the wonderful things you've done for me and who you are. It is such a privilege and honor to know you and be your child.

Today's Scriptures: Ps. 33:1; Ps. 97:12; 1 Thess. 5:16.

April 21

Today God says, *"Do not worry."*

He promises me: "Be careful for nothing; but in every thing by prayer and supplication with thanksgiving let your requests be made known unto God. And the peace of God, which passeth all understanding, shall keep your hearts and minds through Christ Jesus" (Phil. 4:6-7).

My response to the Word: God does not want me to worry. In fact, He invites me to cast all my cares upon Him. He commands me not to worry, and then points out the way to avoid worrying — prayer and supplication with thanksgiving. Worry can't change the past, and it has little effect on the future, but it sure does mess up the present. Therefore, I will give my worries to God and not take them back.

My prayer: Heavenly Father, I thank you that you are the great Burden-bearer in my life. I do not have to carry my burdens by myself. You have invited me to give my worries to you, and this I do now. Thank you for giving me a peace that surpasses all understanding.

Today's Scriptures: Rom. 15:33; Eph. 2:14; Phil. 4:7; 1 Pet. 5:7.

April 22

Today God says, *"Let my Word dwell in you richly, in all wisdom."*

He promises me: "Let the word of Christ dwell in you richly in all wisdom; teaching and admonishing one another in psalms and hymns and spiritual songs, singing with grace in your hearts to the Lord. And whatsoever ye do in word or deed, do all in the name of the Lord Jesus, giving thanks to God and the Father by him" (Col. 3:16-17).

My response to the Word: God's Word imparts spiritual life and faith to me. "So then faith cometh by hearing, and hearing by the word of God." I will walk in the light of God's Word throughout this day. Whatever I do today I will do in the name of my Lord Jesus Christ, with great thanksgiving in my heart. The Bible, unlike all other books, is a book that makes men. Other books are made by men. I will let God's Word dwell within me richly throughout this day.

My prayer: Lord, thank you for your Word which imparts wisdom, faith, and joy to me. I will let it guide everything I do today.

Today's Scriptures: Rom. 10:17; Eph. 6:17; Phil. 2:16.

April 23

Today God says, "*Present your body a living sacrifice to Me.*"

He promises me: "I beseech you therefore, brethren, by the mercies of God, that ye present your bodies a living sacrifice, holy, acceptable unto God, which is your reasonable service [worship]. And be not conformed to this world: but be ye transformed by the renewing of your mind, that ye may prove what is that good, and acceptable, and perfect, will of God" (Rom. 12:1-2).

My response to the Word: With the Lord's help, I will obey Him throughout this day. I start by presenting my body a living sacrifice unto Him because I know this is my reasonable service of worship in light of His many mercies to me. I will resist all conformity to this world-system, and I will cooperate in my spiritual transformation by allowing my mind to be renewed by the Word of God. This, I realize, will enable me to prove God's good, acceptable, and perfect will in my life.

My prayer: Lord, thank you for all your mercies in my life. I give you my life. Take my life and let it be consecrated to you in every aspect. Use me throughout this day, Father.

Today's Scriptures: 1 Cor. 6:20; 1 Cor. 7:23; Phil. 4:18.

April 24

Today God says, *"Faith comes through hearing My Word."*

He promises me: "So then faith cometh by hearing, and hearing by the word of God" (Rom. 10:17).

My response to the Word: Faith is a vitally important part of my life. God says that I am to "live by faith." In order to build my faith I know I must spend time in God's Word. This strengthens me and it renews my mind. Throughout this day I will seek to build my faith by letting my mind be washed continually by the water of God's Word. I recognize that studying the Bible is a privilege, not a duty, and I will walk in the light of God's Word wherever I go.

My prayer: Lord, thank you for your Word which builds my faith and keeps me from sin. I will let it be my weapon in spiritual warfare throughout this day.

Today's Scriptures: Rom. 10:8; Rom. 14:23; 2 Cor. 5:7; Gal 3:11; Eph. 5:26; Eph. 6:17.

April 25

Today God says, *"The weapons of your warfare are mighty."*

He promises me: "For the weapons of our warfare are not carnal, but mighty through God to the pulling down of strong holds; Casting down imaginations, and every high thing that exalteth itself against the knowledge of God, and bringing into captivity every thought to the obedience of Christ" (2 Cor. 10:4-5).

My response to the Word: When waging spiritual warfare, I will remember God's promise to me. I do not have to fight the good fight of faith with fleshly weapons. God has provided me with His Word, the name of Jesus, the word of my testimony, and the blood of Jesus as effective and mighty weapons of spiritual warfare. I will use these weapons throughout this day whenever I encounter temptation or assaults of the enemy. With God's help I will not yield to temptation and I will win each battle.

My prayer: Heavenly Father, thank you for your Word which is sharper than any two-edged sword. Thank you for the precious blood of Jesus and His mighty name. Throughout this day I will wear the armor you've given to me, and I will employ the weapons of spiritual warfare as you've directed me to do.

Today's Scriptures: Eph. 6:11-19; Heb. 4:12; Rev. 12:11.

April 26

Today God says, *"Walk in the light."*

He promises me: "But if we walk in the light, as he is in the light, we have fellowship one with another, and the blood of Jesus Christ his Son cleanseth us from all sin" (1 John 1:7).

My response to the Word: I will walk in the light throughout this day. God is the light of my life. His Word is "a lamp unto my feet, and a light unto my path." I will let the light of His Word guide me throughout this day. The properties of light include healing, cleansing, warmth, energy, illumination, purification, and the eradication of all darkness. I will let the light of God bring these qualities into my life today.

My prayer: Father of lights, in whom there is no variableness or shadow of turning, I present my life to you this day. Thank you for your light which guides me, cleanses me, and dispels all darkness. I will walk in the sunlight of your Word and your love throughout this day.

Today's Scriptures: Ps. 119:105; Eph. 5:8; 1 John 1:7; James 1:17.

April 27

Today God says, *"I will continue the work I've begun in your life."*

He promises me: "Being confident of this very thing, that he which hath begun a good work in you will perform it until the day of Jesus Christ" (Phil. 1:6).

My response to the Word: God is the Potter; I am the clay. He is shaping me and molding me after His will. I will let the Lord have His way in my life throughout this day as I wait before Him, yielded and still. The Word of God proclaims, "But now, O Lord, thou art our father; we are the clay, and thou our potter; and we all are the work of thy hand." I will remember the truth of this prophetic prayer today.

My prayer: Father, thank you for being the Potter in my life. Continue your workmanship so that I can truly become more like Jesus. Have your own way in my life. I surrender myself to you. Mold me and shape me according to your will and your pleasure.

Today's Scriptures: Isa. 64:8; Eph. 2:10; Phil. 2:13; Heb. 13:21.

April 28

Today God says, *"I never change."*

He promises me: "For I am the Lord, I change not" (Mal. 3:6).

My response to the Word: Someone once said, "The only thing that is truly constant is change." I live in a changing world. Values and behaviors seemingly change almost overnight. Circumstances in my daily life change constantly. The thing that gives me stability in such a changing environment is the knowledge that God and His Word never change. The Word of God is the anchor of my soul even when winds and storms swirl around me.

My prayer: Heavenly Father, thank you for your eternal nature which never changes, and for your Word which abides forever. I cling to you and I take my stand upon your Word, and this gives me security every minute of this day.

　　Today's Scriptures:　Heb. 13:8; James 1:17; 2 Pet. 3:8.

April 29

Today God says, *"Jesus is present when two or three believers gather in His name."*

　　He promises me: "For where two or three are gathered together in my name, there am I in the midst of them" (Matt. 18:20).

　　My response to the Word: The power of spiritual unity and agreement is dynamic, and I will endeavor to have fellowship with other believers throughout this day. I will pray with my brothers and sisters, realizing that when we meet together God's power is unleashed. Being with other believers involves the presence of the Lord, because we share His life when we meet together. I will take advantage of every opportunity to enjoy God's presence with other believers today.

　　My prayer: Thank you for the promises of your Word, Father. It is thrilling to know that you are always present when I meet with other believers in the name of Jesus.

　　Today's Scriptures: Ps. 16:11; Ps. 100; 1 Thess. 2:19.

April 30

Today God says, *"There is power in agreeing prayer."*

He promises me: "Again I say unto you, That if two of you shall agree on earth as touching any thing that they shall ask, it shall be done for them of my Father which is in heaven" (Matt. 18:19).

My response to the Word: This powerful prayer promise is one that I shall remember all day long. Through a prayer partnership with another believer, I expect great things to happen. I believe in the power of prayer to effect changes in my life, the lives of others, and circumstances that surround me. When I pray, I will pray with faith in the promises of God's Word. My Father wants to bless me; I will trust and obey Him at all times.

My prayer: Heavenly Father, thank you for promising so many good things to me. I will agree with my prayer partner with absolute confidence in your Word. I know that praying according to your will (your Word) will bring great blessings to me and others.

Today's Scriptures: John 17:21; Acts 6:4; Rom. 12:12.

May 1

Today God says, *"I have redeemed you from the hand of the enemy."*

He promises me: "O give thanks unto the Lord, for he is good: for his mercy endureth for ever. Let the redeemed of the Lord say so, whom he hath redeemed from the hand of the enemy" (Ps. 107:1-2).

My response to the Word: God has redeemed me from the hand of the enemy. Satan is a defeated foe. I no longer live in the kingdom of darkness; I live in the Kingdom of God. Satan had me bound, but Jesus set me free. Therefore, I will obey His Word which tells me to, "Stand fast therefore in the liberty wherewith Christ hath made us free, and be not entangled again with the yoke of bondage." Throughout this day I will stand fast, and I will tell others about the Lord's redemption in my life.

My prayer: Thank you, Lord, for redeeming me. Your Son, my Savior, Jesus Christ, paid the price for me. His blood cleanses me from all sin. I will walk in spiritual freedom throughout this day.

Today's Scriptures: Gal. 5:1; Eph. 1:7; Col. 1:13-14; 1 John 1:7.

May 2

Today God says, *"I want your joy to be full."*

He promises me: "And these things write we unto you, that your joy may be full" (1 John 1:4).

My response to the Word: I have fullness of joy because of the full realization that God has given me life — abundant and eternal life. Joy floods my being when I realize that I can have fellowship with my heavenly Father and my Lord and Savior, Jesus Christ. The joy I experience as a result of knowing Jesus Christ is not based on the circumstances of my life; it is an internal well of blessing from which I will draw throughout this day. "The joy of the Lord is my strength." God's kingdom is righteousness, peace and joy in the Holy Spirit.

My prayer: Lord, I thank you for giving me fullness of joy. This truly is the strength of my life. The joy you've given to me goes far beyond anything this world has to offer. I will walk in your joy today. Fill me with all joy and peace in believing, that I may abound in hope through the power of the Holy Spirit.

Today's Scriptures: Neh. 8:10; John 16:24; Rom. 14:17; Rom. 15:13; 1 Pet. 1:8.

May 3

Today God says, *"Confess your sins, and I will forgive you."*

He promises me: "If we confess our sins, he is faithful and just to forgive us our sins, and to cleanse us from all unrighteousness" (1 John 1:9).

My response to the Word: What a wonderful promise this is. God wants me to confess my sins to Him because He knows that unconfessed sin will fester in my life, causing increasing problems, pain, and turmoil. My Father's faithfulness to me stems from His great love for me. How thankful I am that He has cleansed me from all unrighteousness. God's forgiveness is the key that unlocks the door of resentment and the handcuffs of hatred in my life. It is a power that breaks the chains of bitterness and the shackles of selfishness. It restores me to life.

My prayer: Lord, I know you are faithful to me, and I thank you for your promise that you will forgive me when I confess my sins to you. I confess the following sins to you: _____

_____

_____. Thank you for forgiving and cleansing me.

Today's Scriptures: Ps. 32:5; James 5:16; 1 John 4:15.

May 4

Today God says, *"Love not the world."*

He promises me: "Love not the world, neither the things that are in the world. If any man love the world, the love of the Father is not in him" (1 John 2:15).

My response to the Word: The world and the things of the world used to hold appeal to me, but since I came to know Jesus these things mean very little to me. Throughout this day I will remember the words of my Lord Jesus who said, "But seek ye first the kingdom of God, and his righteousness; and all these things shall be added unto you." As I obey this commandment, I know that everything else will be taken care of.

My prayer: Lord God, thank you for weaning me away from the things of this world. Throughout this day I will put you first, and I will seek your righteousness. Thank you for all the blessings you have given to me.

Today's Scriptures: Matt. 6:33; 1 John 2:16; 1 John 2:17.

May 5

Today God says, *"All authority has been given to Me in heaven and in earth."*

He promises me: "All power [authority] is given unto me in heaven and in earth" (Matt. 28:18).

My response to the Word: All spiritual authority resides in Jesus Christ, and He has taken up residence within me. Therefore, all power in heaven and in earth resides within me. Greater is He that is in me than he that is in the world. I will call upon and draw upon the power of Christ within me throughout this day. His power and authority are for my daily living, and I claim His promise of empowerment for my life this day. It is this power that will enable me to be an effective witness for Jesus Christ.

My prayer: Lord God, thank you for manifesting your power through your Son, Jesus Christ, my Lord, and for empowering me with His indwelling presence. I will walk in His power and strength throughout this day.

Today's Scriptures: Matt. 28:19-20; Acts 1:8; Eph. 3:16-17; 1 John 4:4.

May 6

Today God says, *"I will be with you always."*

He promises me: "Lo, I am with you alway, even unto the end of the world. Amen" (Matt. 28:20).

My response to the Word: Jesus is always with me. I am in Him, and He is in me. His abiding presence, through the power of the Holy Spirit, keeps me going. How I cling to His wonderful promise that He will be with me forever, even unto the end of the world. This important statement formed the final part of Jesus' farewell address to His disciples. It is the last line in His charge to them — the Great Commission. The fact that Jesus rose again and is alive today makes all the difference in the world.

My prayer: Heavenly Father, I believe your Word. It is a treasure-chest of truth and life to me. It is so wonderful to know that Jesus will be with me throughout this day. I choose to walk in His presence, drawing upon His power, each moment. Thank you, Father.

Today's Scriptures: Ps. 16:11; Ps. 95:2; 1 Thess. 2:19; Heb. 13:5.

May 7

Today God says, *"I have chosen you."*

He promises me: "Ye have not chosen me, but I have chosen you, and ordained you, that ye should go and bring forth fruit, and that your fruit should remain: that whatsoever ye shall ask of the Father in my name, he may give it you" (John 15:16).

My response to the Word: In this verse, Jesus promises me several things: (1) He has chosen me. I am His choice. I did not choose Him, but He chose me. (2) The reason He chose me was to bring forth fruit for Him. It will be good fruit and lasting fruit. (3) He wants me to use His name in prayer so that the Father will grant my requests. Throughout this day I will endeavor to be a fruit-bearing Christian and I will pray in the name of Jesus.

My prayer: In the name of Jesus, I ask you, Father, to help me produce the fruit of the Holy

Spirit in all the relationships and responsibilities of my life. How thankful I am, Lord, that Jesus chose me to be His follower.

Today's Scriptures: Gal. 5:22-23; Eph. 1:5; Eph. 1:11.

May 8

Today God says, *"Don't let your heart be troubled."*

He promises me: "Let not your heart be troubled: you believe in God, believe also in me" (John 14:1).

My response to the Word: I will walk in faith throughout this day, because I know that when I believe in God and His Son, Jesus Christ, my heart will no longer be worried or troubled. I believe the words of Jesus who said, "Peace I leave with you, my peace I give unto you: not as the world giveth, give I unto you. Let not your heart be troubled, neither let it be afraid." Experiencing the peace Jesus gives lifts me above my problems.

My prayer: Heavenly Father, thank you for giving abiding peace to me through faith in Jesus Christ. I will remain focused on you throughout this day, because I know this is the source of perfect peace in my life.

Today's Scriptures: Isa. 26:3; John 14:27; Phil. 4:6-8; 1 Pet. 5:7.

May 9

Today God says, *"Keep your mind stayed on Me."*

He promises me: "Thou wilt keep him in perfect peace, whose mind is stayed on thee: because he trusteth in thee" (Isa. 26:3).

My response to the Word: In order to experience God's perfect peace throughout this day I must keep my mind stayed on Him and I must trust Him. It is not hard to trust the Lord because of His great faithfulness in my life. He has always supplied all my needs. Perhaps the hardest part is keeping my mind stayed on Him due to all the distractions in the world around me. Nonetheless, I will keep focused on the Lord. The Bible says, ". . . let us lay aside every weight, and the sin which doth so easily beset us, and let us run with patience the race that is set before us, Looking unto Jesus the author and finisher of our faith." I will keep looking to Jesus throughout this day.

My prayer: Heavenly Father, thank you for the marvelous peace you have imparted to me. By your grace I will trust you and keep my mind focused on you and let your peace rule in my heart throughout this day.

Today's Scriptures: Ps. 46:10; Phil. 4:8; Col. 3:15; Heb. 12:1-2.

May 10

Today God says, *"I am your light and your salvation."*

He promises me: "The Lord is my light and my salvation; whom shall I fear? the Lord is the strength of my life; of whom shall I be afraid?" (Ps. 27:1).

My response to the Word: Because God is my light and my salvation, I never need to fear anyone or anything. His perfect love casts out all fear in my life. The Apostle John wrote, "There is no fear in love; but perfect love casteth out fear: because fear hath torment. He that feareth is not made perfect in love."

My prayer: Lord, with your help I will walk in your light and love throughout this day. Because I know you I have nothing to fear. Thank you, Father.

Today's Scriptures: Mic. 7:8; John 8:12; 1 John 4:18.

May 11

Today God says, *"Whatever you do shall prosper."*

He promises me: "And he shall be like a tree planted by the rivers of water, that bringeth forth his fruit in his season; his leaf also shall not wither; and whatsoever he doeth shall prosper" (Ps. 1:3).

My response to the Word: This precious promise is extended to those who walk not in the counsel of the ungodly and do not stand in the way of sinners. When I delight in God's law (His Word), and meditate upon the Scriptures, I will become like a mighty oak tree, prosperous and strong, withstanding every storm of life. I will be a fruitful Christian who possesses life and vitality, and whatever I do will prosper. This is God's promise to *me*.

My prayer: Dear Father, I draw close to you as I meditate in your Word and consider the magnitude of your promises to me. It amazes me to realize how much you love me and want to bless me. Thank you, Father.

Today's Scriptures: Josh. 1:8; Isa. 48:15; 3 John 2.

May 12

Today God says, *"My blessing is upon you."*

He promises me: "Salvation belongeth unto the Lord: thy blessing is upon thy people" (Ps. 3:8).

My response to the Word: God has already put His blessing upon me; it is not something I have to watch and wait for because it is already there! This realization leads me into thanksgiving and praise. There is so much to be thankful for. I am thankful that God supplies everything I need in every way, and His blessing is upon me. God's great salvation includes eternal life, being His child, deliverance from the power of darkness, preservation, provision, healing, and wholeness.

My prayer: Heavenly Father, you are the greatest blessing in my life, and from you all blessings flow. Thank you for everything you are to me.

Today's Scriptures: Ps. 24:5; Phil. 4:19; Col. 1:12-14; 1 Thess. 5:23; 1 John 3:1-2.

May 13

Today God says, *"I have set you apart for Myself."*

He promises me: "But know that the Lord hath set apart him that is godly for himself: the Lord will hear when I call unto him" (Ps. 4:3).

My response to the Word: God has sanctified me and set me apart for himself. He promises to hear my prayers. I realize the truth of this saying: "It is not always the most talented people who serve the Lord best — it is the consecrated ones." Throughout this day, I will realize that God has consecrated me — set me apart — for His service, and I will be happy in the service of my King.

My prayer: Take my life and let it be consecrated, Lord, to you. Take every part of my life and use me in your service. Thank you, Lord, for setting me apart and promising to hear and answer my prayers.

Today's Scriptures: Ezek. 20:12; John 17:17; Eph. 5:26.

May 14

Today God says, *"I am your defense."*

He promises me: "My defence is of God, which saveth the upright in heart" (Ps. 7:10).

My response to the Word: I have surrendered my right to self-defense, because I know that God is my defense. He promises to defend me from evil, my enemies, those who persecute me, Satan, and all opposition. The Word declares, "Dearly beloved, avenge not yourselves, but rather give place unto wrath: for it is written, Vengeance is mine; I will repay, saith the Lord." I will obey the Word of God.

My prayer: Lord, thank you for your Word which shows me how to conduct my life in every way. I yield my right to self-defense to you because I know you will defend me.

Today's Scriptures: Ps. 59:9; Ps. 91:15; Rom. 12:19.

May 15

Today God says, *"Draw near to Me, and I will draw near to you."*

He promises me: "Draw nigh to God, and he will draw nigh to you. Cleanse your hands, ye sinners; and purify your hearts, ye double minded" (James 4:8).

My response to the Word: This is an important spiritual principle for me to remember throughout this day: God will come to me if I will go to Him. The closer I get to Him, the closer He gets to me. By God's grace I will walk closer to the Lord today than I have ever walked before. I will live in His presence through prayer, worship, thanksgiving, and praise.

My prayer: Heavenly Father, thank you for your promise that you will draw near to me if I will draw near to you. It is so good to be close to you, and I will seek to get nearer to you throughout this day.

Today's Scriptures: Song of Sol. 1:4; John 6:44; Heb. 10:22.

May 16

Today God says, *"Resist the devil, and he will flee from you."*

He promises me: "Submit yourselves therefore to God. Resist the devil, and he will flee from you" (James 4:7).

My response to the Word: The key to resisting the devil is found in the commandment, "Submit yourselves therefore to God." I will walk in submission to the Lord throughout this day, then, when I resist the devil, I know he will flee from me. I will also remember that Satan doesn't care what I worship as long as I don't worship God. God will have first place in my life throughout this day.

My prayer: Dear Lord, thank you for giving me the ability to submit to you. I do so now, Lord, and I will continue to submit to you throughout this day. It is wonderful to know that the devil will flee from me when I resist him.

Today's Scriptures: Eph. 4:27; Eph. 6:11; 1 Pet. 5:8.

May 17

Today God says, *"I have reserved an incorruptible inheritance in heaven for you."*

He promises me: "Blessed be the God and Father of our Lord Jesus Christ, which according to his abundant mercy hath begotten us again unto a lively hope by the resurrection of Jesus Christ from the dead. To an inheritance incorruptible, and undefiled, and that fadeth not away, reserved in heaven for you" (1 Pet. 1:3-4).

My response to the Word: As a believer, I have so much to look forward to. Jesus has already prepared a place for me in heaven. I like what one man said about the believer's eternal destiny: "If you wish to dwell in the house of many mansions, you must make your reservation in advance." Through faith, I have placed my trust in Christ for salvation, and He promises me that He has reserved an incorruptible and unfading inheritance in heaven for me.

My prayer: Lord God, thank you for the wonderful promise of heaven. I look forward to spending all eternity in your presence, and I will begin by living in your presence today.

Today's Scriptures: John 14:1-4; Eph. 1:11; Col. 1:12.

May 18

Today God says, *"Love one another as I have loved you."*

He promises me: "A new commandment I give unto you, That ye love one another; as I have loved you, that ye also love one another. By this shall all men know that ye are my disciples, if ye have love one to another" (John 13:34-35).

My response to the Word: The greatest commandment of all is the commandment to love. Jesus wants me to love God with all my heart, soul, strength, and mind, and to love my neighbor as I love myself. The ability to give such love to God and others stems directly from the fact that Jesus first loved me. "We love him, because he first loved us." His love has been shed abroad in my heart by the Holy Spirit. I will walk in love throughout this day.

My prayer: Lord, thank you for your love which enables me to love others. Help me to love others as you have loved me throughout this day.

Today's Scriptures: Matt. 22:37-39; Luke 10:27; John 14:15; Rom. 5:5; 1 John 4:19.

May 19

Today God says, *"My Word is settled forever in heaven."*

He promises me: "For ever, O Lord, thy word is settled in heaven. Thy faithfulness is unto all generations: thou hast established the earth, and it abideth" (Ps. 119:89-90).

My response to the Word: The Word of God is a solid rock on which I stand. I take my stand upon the Word today, realizing that all other ground is sinking sand. God's Word never changes, and I know I can depend upon His Word throughout this day. Three great sins of this age are indifference to, neglect of, and disrespect for the Word of God. I choose to make the Bible my rule for faith and living throughout this day.

My prayer: Lord, thank you for your Word which is forever settled in heaven. I treasure your Word, and I will live according to its promises and precepts throughout this day.

Today's Scriptures: Ps. 18:30; Ps. 107:20; John 1:1.

May 20

Today God says, *"There is no condemnation when you walk in the Spirit."*

He promises me: "There is therefore now no condemnation to them which are in Christ Jesus, who walk not after the flesh, but after the Spirit" (Rom. 8:1).

My response to the Word: I will walk in the Spirit throughout this day. In so doing, I know I will avoid all condemnation. Condemnation comes when a person walks in the flesh. I will remember these words of the Apostle Paul: "For they that are after the flesh do mind the things of the flesh; but they that are after the Spirit the things of the Spirit. For to be carnally minded is death; but to be spiritually minded is life and peace."

My prayer: Lord, thank you for freeing me from the condemnation that comes from fleshly living. You have given me a completely new perspective, and I choose the spiritual-mindedness that enables me to experience your life and peace this day. With your help, I will walk in the Spirit each step of the way.

Today's Scriptures: John 8:11; Rom. 8:5-6; 1 John 3:21.

May 21

Today God says, *"Let My Spirit lead you."*

He promises me: "For as many as are led by the Spirit of God, they are the sons of God" (Rom. 8:14).

My response to the Word: I want to be led by God's Holy Spirit every moment of every day because it is an exciting adventure to walk with Him. He will guide me each step of the way. He empowers me to live a life that is pleasing to God. "But if the Spirit of him that raised up Jesus from the dead dwell in you, he that raised up Christ from the dead shall also quicken your mortal bodies by the Spirit that dwelleth in you." I will let the Spirit of God lead me and fill me throughout this day.

My prayer: Heavenly Father, thank you for giving me your Holy Spirit. Fill me continuously with your Spirit so that I will be able to follow His leading throughout this day.

Today's Scriptures: Rom. 8:11; 1 Cor. 3:16; Gal. 5:16; Gal. 5:25; Eph. 5:18.

May 22

Today God says, *"I am for you; therefore, nothing can be against you."*

He promises me: "What shall we then say to these things? If God be for us, who can be against us?" (Rom. 8:31).

My response to the Word: God is for me. Because this is true, nothing that is against me can touch me throughout this day. I know God is for me; His Word declares His faithfulness to me on nearly every page. As someone has said, "God is not only a present help in time of trouble, but also a great help in keeping us out of trouble." God is for me, and I will be for Him throughout this day.

My prayer: Lord, thank you for being for me, and for your promise that because you are for me, nothing shall be able to be against me. I claim this promise by faith for my life today.

Today's Scriptures: Ps. 16:11; Ps. 46:1; 1 Thess. 2:19.

May 23

Today God says, *"The Word is near you; it is even in your mouth and in your heart."*

He promises me: "But what saith it? The word is nigh thee, even in thy mouth, and in thy heart: that is the word of faith, which we preach" (Rom. 10:8).

My response to the Word: The Word of God is always near me. I have hid it in my heart in order to avoid sin. I will keep it in my mouth. I will speak its faith-filled principles and promises to my own heart, and this will build faith within me to appropriate His promises. I will speak the Word to the enemy, and he will flee. I will speak the Word to others, and they will be encouraged. I will walk in the light of God's Word today.

My prayer: Thank you, Father, for your Word which is in my mouth and in my heart. I will memorize it, meditate upon it, pray it, believe it, obey it, and live it throughout this day.

Today's Scriptures: Ps. 119:11; Luke 4; Rom. 10:17.

May 24

Today God says, *"I will rebuke the devourer for your sake."*

He promises me: "And I will rebuke the devourer for your sakes, and he shall not destroy the fruits of your ground; neither shall your vine cast her fruit before the time in the field, saith the Lord of hosts" (Mal. 3:11).

My response to the Word: God assures me that my life will be fruitful if I will walk in trust and obedience before Him. The devil (the devourer) will not be able to touch me because God, my loving Father, will rebuke him for my sake. I take great heart in this promise because I know God wants to bless me, keep me, and make my way prosperous.

My prayer: Dear Lord, thank you for protecting me from the evil one, and for rebuking him when he attempts to devour all you have given to me. I rejoice over the fact that the enemy is a defeated foe.

Today's Scriptures: Zech. 3:2; Matt. 17:18; Luke 9:42.

May 25

Today God says, *"The gates of hell will not prevail against My Church."*

He promises me: ". . . upon this rock I will build my church; and the gates of hell shall not prevail against it" (Matt. 16:18).

My response to the Word: The Church of Jesus Christ is firmly founded on the solid rock of God's living Word — Jesus Christ. He is the chief cornerstone. He has defeated the devil, "having spoiled principalities and powers, he made a shew of them openly, triumphing over them in it." The Father has given Jesus all authority in heaven and in earth, and He has delegated that authority to His church. As a member of Christ's church, the gates of hell shall not prevail against me.

My prayer: Father, thank you for giving me membership in your family — the Church of Jesus Christ. Thank you, also, for protecting your Church throughout the centuries and for your promise that the gates of hell shall not prevail against it.

Today's Scriptures: Matt. 28:18; Eph. 1:22; Eph. 2:20; Col. 2:15.

May 26

Today God says, *"I have given you a spirit of power, love, and a sound mind."*

He promises me: "For God hath not given us the spirit of fear; but of power, and of love, and of a sound mind" (2 Tim. 1:7).

My response to the Word: God has imparted a new spirit to me in place of the old spirit of fear. He has renewed my spirit into one that is full of power and love. In place of worry and anxiety, He has given me a sound mind. "There is no fear in love; but perfect love casteth out fear: because fear hath torment. He that feareth is not made perfect in love." Fear no longer has any place in my life at all.

My prayer: Lord, thank you for the spirit of love and power that gives me a sound mind as I go about my daily activities. Let your Spirit govern all that I do today.

Today's Scriptures: Rom. 8:15; 1 John 4:11; 1 John 4:18.

May 27

Today God says, *"Be strong in the grace that is in Christ Jesus."*

He promises me: "Thou therefore, my son, be strong in the grace that is in Christ Jesus" (2 Tim. 2:1).

My response to the Word: In writing these words of spiritual direction to young Timothy, the Apostle Paul is preparing him for what he knows will come. He goes on, "And the things that thou hast heard of me among many witnesses, the same commit thou to faithful men, who shall be able to teach others also. Thou therefore endure hardness as a good soldier of Jesus Christ." I will remember these important words throughout this day as I endeavor, with God's help to be strong in the grace that is in Christ Jesus.

My prayer: Lord, thank you for the grace which is in Christ Jesus, a grace that enables me to endure hardness as a good soldier of Jesus Christ. Thank you for His strength which helps me to face every challenge. I will walk in His grace throughout this day.

Today's Scriptures: Eph. 2:8-9; 2 Tim. 2:2-3; 1 Pet. 4:10.

May 28

Today God says, *"Study to show yourself approved unto Me."*

He promises me: "Study to shew thyself approved unto God, a workman that needeth not to be ashamed, rightly dividing the word of truth" (2 Tim. 2:15).

My response to the Word: I desire to be God's workman; therefore, I will study His Word diligently so that I will never have to be ashamed because I will understand His truth. His Word is truth. His truth sets me free, and it sanctifies me. I will memorize His Word, meditate upon its liberating truths, walk in its light, and rightly divide it throughout this day.

My prayer: Heavenly Father, I love your Word. It give me faith, life, hope, and strength. I will walk in its light today.

Today's Scriptures: John 8:32; John 17:17; Acts 17:11.

May 29

Today God says, *"You have eternal life."*

He promises me: "And this is life eternal, that they might know thee the only true God, and Jesus Christ, whom thou hast sent" (John 17:3).

My response to the Word: Because I know God and His Son, Jesus Christ, I know I have eternal life. I want to know God better, and throughout this day I will seek to know Him, whom to know aright is life eternal. "And this is the record, that God hath given to us eternal life, and this life is in his Son. He that hath the Son hath life; and he that hath not the Son of God hath not life."

My prayer: Loving Father, thank you for giving me eternal life through Jesus Christ, my Lord. It is so liberating and empowering to know that I will never perish, but live forever with you.

Today's Scriptures: John 3:16; John 17:2-3; Titus 1:2; 1 John 5:11-12.

May 30

Today God says, *"If you ask anything according to My will, I will hear your prayer."*

He promises me: "And this is the confidence that we have in him, that, if we ask any thing according to his will, he heareth us: And if we know that he hear us, whatsoever we ask, we know that we have the petitions that we desired of him" (1 John 5:14-15).

My response to the Word: God hears my prayers when I pray according to His will. His will is fully revealed in His Word. Therefore, when I pray according to His Word, and especially when I actually pray His Word, I can be certain that He is hearing my prayer. He promises me, "So shall my word be that goeth forth out of my mouth: it shall not return unto me void, but is shall accomplish that which I please, and it shall prosper in the thing whereto I sent it." God responds to His Word.

My prayer: Father, reveal your will to me in every area of my life so that I will know how to pray accordingly. Thank you for your Word which reveals your will and shows me how to pray.

Today's Scriptures: Isa. 55:11; Rom. 12:2; Eph. 6:6.

May 31

Today God says, *"Seek Me while I may be found, and call upon Me."*

He promises me: "Seek ye the Lord while he may be found, call ye upon him while he is near" (Isa. 55:6).

My response to the Word: I will seek the Lord throughout this day, and I will call upon Him because I know He is near. In fact, I will obey Jesus who said, "But seek ye first the kingdom of God, and his righteousness; and all these things shall be added unto you." God will have first place in my life throughout this day. I will seek Him and His righteousness.

My prayer: Lord God, I praise you for the precious promises of your Word. I know you expect me to live according to them, and this I will do today. I do seek you and call upon you. Thank you for always being there.

Today's Scriptures: Matt. 6:33; Luke 11:9; Rom. 3:11.

June 1

Today God says, *"My kingdom is not meat and drink, but righteousness, peace, and joy in the Holy Spirit."*

He promises me: "For the kingdom of God is not meat and drink; but righteousness, and peace, and joy in the Holy Ghost" (Rom. 14:17).

My response to the Word: God has accepted me into His kingdom where righteousness, peace, and joy in the Holy Spirit form the environment. Jesus is the King of kings and Lord of lords in my life, and I will submit myself to His Lordship throughout this day. The righteousness, peace, and joy I experience in His kingdom make life worthwhile for me.

My prayer: Father, thank you for your gifts of righteousness, peace, and joy which enable me to experience full kingdom-living in the here-and-now. I will walk in those attributes throughout this day as I submit to the Lordship of Jesus Christ.

Today's Scriptures: John 18:36; 1 Cor. 4:20; Rev. 19:16.

June 2

Today God says, *"No one has seen or heard all that I have prepared for you."*

He promises me: "Eye hath not seen, nor ear heard, neither have entered into the heart of man, the things which God hath prepared for them that love him. But God hath revealed them unto us by his Spirit: for the Spirit searcheth all things, yea, the deep things of God" (1 Cor. 2:9-10).

My response to the Word: As I contemplate this Scripture, I realize that God has already prepared so many wonderful things for me. By His Spirit He continuously reveals these deeper things to me. Indeed, He has already blessed me with every spiritual blessing in heavenly places in Christ. I will walk in His blessings throughout this day.

My prayer: Father in heaven, thank you for all that you have prepared for me. I realize that I know only a small part of this at present, but I trust you to continue to reveal the truth to me. I love you, Lord.

Today's Scriptures: John 14:1-6; Eph. 1:3; Rev. 4.

June 3

Today God says, *"My Kingdom is not in word; it is in power."*

He promises me: "For the kingdom of God is not in word, but in power" (1 Cor. 4:20).

My response to the Word: The Kingdom of God is the most powerful kingdom that has ever existed, and its power is available to me. I will walk in the power of the Kingdom of God throughout this day. God is not only an ever-present help in times of trouble, but He is also the power that keeps me out of trouble. As I submit to Him, His power keeps me from sin and evil, and it enables me to walk in victory as an effective witness for Jesus Christ.

My prayer: Thank you for the power of your Kingdom, Father. Throughout this day I will remain cognizant of the fact that you are supplying me with the strength and power I need for every challenge that comes my way.

Today's Scriptures: 1 Cor. 1:24; 2 Cor. 6:7; Eph. 1:19.

June 4

Today God says, *"You are one spirit with Me."*

He promises me: "But he that is joined unto the Lord is one spirit" (1 Cor. 6:17).

My response to the Word: Jesus said, "I am the true vine, and my Father is the husbandman. Every branch in me that beareth not fruit he taketh away: and every branch that beareth fruit, he purgeth it, that it may bring forth more fruit. . . . Abide in me, and I in you." I will abide in the Lord throughout this day because I know that I have been joined to Him, and this is the key to fruitfulness in my life.

My prayer: Lord, I realize that without Jesus Christ I can do nothing. I am joined unto the Lord. Therefore, I will abide in Him throughout this day.

Today's Scriptures: John 14:5; John 15:1-4; John 17:23.

June 5

Today God says, *"I want My love to fill your heart through the Holy Spirit."*

He promises me: "And hope maketh not ashamed; because the love of God is shed abroad in our hearts by the Holy Ghost which is given unto us" (Rom. 5:5).

My response to the Word: Knowing God fills my life with hope. His love is shed abroad in my heart by the Holy Spirit. These two facts make all the difference in the world to me. Someone has said, "Love is the fairest flower that blooms in God's garden." Throughout this day, therefore, I will walk in the aroma of God's love, and as I breathe in His spiritual power I know I will be filled with hope.

My prayer: Thank you, Father, for filling me with your Holy Spirit who spreads your love throughout my innermost being. I will walk in your love throughout this day.

Today's Scriptures: Eph. 2:4; 2 Thess. 2:16; 1 John 4:10.

June 6

Today God says, *"I have made Jesus Christ to be sin for you so that you could become My righteousness."*

He promises me: "For he hath made him to be sin for us, who knew no sin; that we might be made the righteousness of God in him" (2 Cor. 5:21).

My response to the Word: What amazing metamorphoses are revealed in this passage. Jesus Christ, the Son of God, who was totally without sin, became sin on the cross of Calvary. He took all of my sin upon Him. Because He willingly did this, I am now clothed in God's righteousness. The righteousness of Christ has been imparted to me. What a staggering thought this is — Christ knew no sin, but He became sin for me. I have no righteousness within myself, but because of Jesus' death, I have been made the righteousness of God in Him. I will walk in God's righteousness throughout this day.

My prayer: Thank you, Lord, for sending Jesus Christ to die for my sins so that His righteousness could be imparted to me. Help me to walk in the righteousness of Christ throughout this day.

Today's Scriptures: Zeph. 2:3; Gal. 2:21; Eph. 6:14.

June 7

Today God says, *"I love a cheerful giver."*

He promises me: "Every man according as he purposeth in his heart, so let him give; not grudgingly, or of necessity: for God loveth a cheerful giver" (2 Cor. 9:7).

My response to the Word: God has given so much to me, and I want to give as much as I can back to Him. Throughout this day, therefore, I will remember the importance of giving cheerfully, realizing that it makes me cheerful to give in the first place. I know that it is more blessed to give than to receive. Two marks of the Christian life are giving and forgiving, and I will cheerfully practice both today.

My prayer: Dear Lord, thank you for blessing me with so much. I will remember that I am a steward over your property, and I will give as you direct me. Thank you for the privilege of giving, Father.

Today's Scriptures: Mal. 3:8-12; Matt. 7:7; Luke 6:38.

June 8

Today God says, *"I am able to make all grace abound toward you."*

He promises me: "And God is able to make all grace abound toward you; that ye, always having all sufficiency in all things, may abound to every good work" (2 Cor. 9:8).

My response to the Word: God wants me to abound in good works. Therefore, He gives me His grace which provides me with everything I need. Truly, His grace is sufficient for me. My heart is filled with wonder and praise as I contemplate His all-sufficient grace in my life. "Thanks be to God for his unspeakable gift."

My prayer: Marvelous Lord, thank you for the working of your marvelous grace in my life. You have given me everything I need, and I praise your holy name.

Today's Scriptures: 2 Cor. 9:15; 2 Cor. 12:9; Eph. 2:8-9.

June 9

Today God says, *"My grace is sufficient for you."*

He promises me: "My grace is sufficient for thee: for my strength is made perfect in weakness. Most gladly therefore will I rather glory in my infirmities, that the power of Christ may rest upon me" (2 Cor. 12:9).

My response to the Word: God's strength is made perfect in my weakness. Therefore, I will let my weaknesses lead me to Him so that I can receive His strength. I know that God's grace is totally sufficient for me. I do not have to walk in my own strength because the power of Christ rests upon me. True greatness does not lie in being strong, but in knowing how to rely on God's strength. I will rely on God's strength throughout this day.

My prayer: God, you are perfectly strong. When I come to the end of my way, I realize that it is a wonderful opportunity to prove your strength. Thank you for your all-sufficient grace which is at work in my life.

Today's Scriptures: Eph. 2:8-9; 2 Thess. 2:16; Titus 2:11.

June 10

Today God says, *"You are crucified with Christ."*

He promises me, "I am crucified with Christ: nevertheless I live; yet not I, but Christ liveth in me: and the life which I now live in the flesh I live by the faith of the Son of God, who loved me, and gave himself for me" (Gal. 2:20).

My response to the Word: Christ died on the cross for me. In fact, I died there with Him. I am crucified with Him. Even so, I am still alive, but now I live by the faith of the Son of God who loved me and gave himself for me. It is Jesus Christ who now lives within me. Throughout this day I will let Him live His life through me.

My prayer: Thank you, Father, for sending Jesus to die for me. It is wonderful to know that

He lives within me. Continuously fill me with
your Spirit so that I will produce the fruit of your
Spirit in all my relationships and responsibilities
this day.

Today's Scriptures: Rom. 6:6; Gal. 5:24; Col. 2:20.

June 11

Today God says, *"Christ has redeemed you from the
Law's curse."*

He promises me: "Christ hath redeemed us
from the curse of the law, being made a curse for
us: for it is written, Cursed is every one that
hangeth on a tree" (Gal. 3:13).

My response to the Word: In his own strength,
no man is capable of keeping all the Law. This is
good in that it teaches us that we need a source of
strength beyond ourselves. The Lord Jesus Christ
redeemed us from the law's curse. Paul wrote,
"Wherefore the law was our schoolmaster to bring
us unto Christ, that we might be justified by
faith." I praise God that I have been justified by
faith in Christ.

My prayer: Dear Lord, thank you for redeeming me from the curse of the Law by bringing me
to Jesus Christ who has redeemed me and justified
me. I love Him with all my heart.

Today's Scriptures: Rom. 8:1-2; Gal. 3:24; Col. 1:14.

June 12

Today God says, *"Stand fast in the liberty with which Christ has made you free."*

He promises me: "Stand fast therefore in the liberty wherewith Christ hath made us free, and be not entangled again with the yoke of bondage" (Gal. 5:1).

My response to the Word: Jesus Christ has set me free from sin and death. He said, "And ye shall know the truth, and the truth shall make you free" This has already happened in my life, because Jesus Christ is the truth. He wants me to stand fast in the freedom He has imparted to me, and to make sure that I will not get entangled again in any yoke of bondage. I will walk in the Lord's freedom throughout this day.

My prayer: Thank you, Father, for setting me free from all guilt, shame, and fear. I will not allow myself to become entangled by these bondages ever again because I know I'm truly free.

Today's Scriptures: John 8:32; John 14:6; Rom. 8:21.

June 13

Today God says, *"Live in the Spirit, and walk in the Spirit."*

He promises me: If we live in the Spirit, let us also walk in the Spirit" (Gal. 5:25).

My response to the Word: Jesus died on the cross; then on the third day He rose from the dead. Before He ascended into heaven He promised, "But the comforter, which is the Holy Ghost, whom the Father will send in my name, he shall teach you all things, and bring all things to your remembrance, whatsoever I have said unto you." He has made it possible for me to live and walk in the Holy Spirit, and I will do so throughout this day.

My prayer: Lord God, thank you for sending your Holy Spirit to teach me all things. I will live and walk in Him today.

Today's Scriptures: John 14:26; Rom. 8:1-2; Gal. 5:16.

June 14

Today God says, *"The just shall live by faith."*

He promises me: "But that no man is justified by the law in the sight of God, it is evident: for, The just shall live by faith. And the law is not of faith" (Gal. 3:11-12).

My response to the Word: Throughout this day I will live by faith, not by sight. I know that it is impossible to please God without faith. "Faith is the substance of things hoped for, the evidence of things not seen." This faith which God imparts to me by His Word justifies me — makes me live just as if I'd never sinned! I will walk in God's faith today.

My prayer: Thank you, Lord, for justifying me through faith. I will live by faith, not by sight, throughout this day.

Today's Scriptures: Rom. 10:17; 2 Cor. 5:7; Heb. 11:1; Heb. 11:6.

June 15

Today God says, *"I have called you unto liberty."*

He promises me: "For, brethren, ye have been called unto liberty; only use not liberty for an occasion to the flesh, but by love serve one another. For all the law is fulfilled in one word, even in this; Thou shalt love thy neighbour as thyself" (Gal. 5:13-14).

My response to the Word: God has called me into spiritual freedom. This glorious liberty is not to be used in a selfish manner, but in love. Love fulfills all the Law. In light of this, therefore, I will walk in love throughout this day. The Bible admonishes me to love my neighbors and my enemies, and I will endeavor to do this throughout this day.

My prayer: Lord God, thank you for the freedom you have given to me. I will walk in your freedom and your love throughout this day.

Today's Scriptures: John 8:32; 2 Cor. 3:17; Gal. 5:1.

June 16

Today God says, *"Walk in the Spirit, and you will not fulfill the lust of the flesh."*

He promises me: "This I say then, Walk in the Spirit, and ye shall not fulfill the lust of the flesh" (Gal. 5:16).

My response to the Word: Though the lusts of the flesh are a given part of the human condition, I do not have to give in to them because God has provided a higher dimension of living. I will walk in His Spirit throughout this day, and this will keep me from fulfilling the lusts of the flesh. I will bear the fruit of the Spirit in all the relationships and responsibilities of my life this day: "But the fruit of the spirit is love, joy, peace, longsuffering, gentleness, goodness, faith, Meekness, temperance: against such there is no law."

My prayer: Heavenly Father, continuously fill me with your Spirit today so that I will be able to walk in your Spirit at all times. I want others to see the fruit of your Spirit in my life so that they will want to taste and see your goodness.

Today's Scriptures: John 14:26; Rom. 8:13; Rom. 8:37.

June 17

Today God says, *"Bear the burdens of others, and fulfill the law of Christ."*

He promises me: "Bear ye one another's burdens, and so fulfill the law of Christ" (Gal. 6:2).

My response to the Word: Paul wrote, "Brethren, if a man be overtaken in a fault, ye which are spiritual, restore such an one in the spirit of meekness; considering thyself, lest thou also be tempted." This admonition is one aspect of helping others to bear their burdens. I will take every opportunity to help others throughout this day, realizing that in so doing I am fulfilling Christ's law which is love. I will walk in love today.

My prayer: Lord God, thank you for each opportunity that comes my way to help others. I realize that when I help someone else I am serving you. Help me to fulfill the law of Christ today.

Today's Scriptures: Rom. 15:1; 1 Cor. 12:31; Gal. 6:1.

June 18

Today God says, *"I have blessed you with all spiritual blessings in heavenly places in Christ."*

He promises me: "Blessed be the God and Father of our Lord Jesus Christ, who hath blessed us with all spiritual blessings in heavenly places in Christ" (Eph. 1:3).

My response to the Word: Praise and thanksgiving are the only appropriate responses to all

God has done in my life. He has already blessed me with every spiritual blessing in heavenly places in Christ. Those spiritual blessings include eternal life, abundant life, His Word, His Spirit, justification, sanctification, victory, prosperity, and so many other wonderful attributes of life in Christ. I am seated with Christ Jesus in the heavenly places, and I will remember this truth all day long.

My prayer: Lord, I bless you, praise you, and thank you for blessing me with so many spiritual blessings in Christ. Thank you for seating me in the heavenly places with Him.

Today's Scriptures: Deut. 28:2; Prov. 10:6; Prov. 28:20.

June 19

Today God says, *"I have raised you up and seated you with Christ Jesus in the heavenly places."*

He promises me: "And hath raised us up together and made us sit together in heavenly places in Christ Jesus: That in the ages to come he might shew the exceeding riches of his grace in his kindness toward us through Christ Jesus" (Eph. 2:6-7).

My response to the Word: God has raised me up to the level where I sit with Christ Jesus in heavenly places. This is true transcendence. The reason He did this was so that He would be able to show the exceeding riches of His grace toward me through Christ Jesus. God's wonderful grace is greater than all my sin, and it enables me to rise above life's circumstances, into a spiritual realm where all is peace and joy.

My prayer: Heavenly Father, thank you for raising me up and seating me with Christ Jesus in the heavenly places. I pray to know fully the exceeding riches of your grace through Christ Jesus.

Today's Scriptures: Eph. 1:3; Eph. 1:11; Eph. 1:19-23.

June 20

Today God says, *"Salvation is My gift to you."*

He promises me: "For by grace are ye saved through faith; and that not of yourselves; it is the gift of God: Not of works, lest any man should boast" (Eph. 2:8-9).

My response to the Word: God has saved me by His grace through faith. His grace is the unmerited favor He has bestowed on my life. I do not deserve His great salvation, but He has chosen to give it to me freely. The Word tells me, "For all have sinned, and come short of the glory of God." Then it proclaims His grace to me: "For the wages of sin is death; but the gift of God is eternal life through Jesus Christ our Lord." I will never forget "the exceeding riches of his grace" that I have so freely received.

My prayer: Heavenly Father, thank you for your grace which saves me from all my sin. I know I have been saved by your grace through faith. Thank you for the gift of eternal life.

Today's Scriptures: Rom. 3:23; Rom. 6:23; Eph. 2:7-10; 1 John 5:13.

June 21

Today God says, *"I am your peace."*

He promises me: "For he is our peace, who hath made both one, and hath broken down the middle wall of partition between us; Having abolished in his flesh the enmity, even the law of commandments contained in ordinances; for to make in himself of twain one new man, so making peace" (Eph. 2:14-15).

My response to the Word: God is my peace. Through Him, I have peace of mind and spiritual peace. I will walk in peace today as I remember this vital admonition: "Let the peace of God rule in your hearts, to the which also ye are called in one body; and be ye thankful." The peace God gives is the only true and lasting peace.

My prayer: God of peace, thank you for being peace to me. With your help I will experience your peace throughout this day.

Today's Scriptures: John 14:27; Phil 4:7; Col. 3:15.

June 22

Today God says, *"In Christ you have boldness and access with confidence."*

He promises me: "According to the eternal purpose which he purposed in Christ Jesus our Lord: In whom we have boldness and access with confidence by the faith of him" (Eph. 3:11-12).

My response to the Word: Faith in Christ, as it is imparted to me through the Word of God, gives me the courage to face the present with confidence, and the future with expectancy. It also helps me to realize that when I go to God in prayer, He will hear me. The Bible says, "Let us therefore come boldly unto the throne of grace, that we may obtain mercy, and find grace to help in time of need."

My prayer: Heavenly Father, thank you for the prayer promises of your Word which clearly show me that you want me to come to you. Thank you for Jesus who gives me access to your throne.

Today's Scriptures: Eph. 3:12; Heb. 4:16; 1 John 3:21; 1 John 5:14.

June 23

Today God says, *"Be strengthened with might by My Spirit in your inner man."*

He promises me: "That he would grant you, according to the riches of his glory, to be strengthened with might by his Spirit in the inner man" (Eph. 3:16).

My response to the Word: God is strengthening me with His might by His Spirit who dwells deep inside of me. This is His desire for me. He has provided a complete and effective way for me to have His spiritual strength. I will avail myself of His power and might by being filled with His Spirit throughout this day, remembering that ". . . if the Spirit of him that raised up Jesus from the dead dwell in you, he that raised up Christ from the dead shall also quicken your mortal bodies by his Spirit that dwelleth in you."

My prayer: Heavenly Father, thank you for imparting your Spirit to me. With His help, I will walk in your strength and might throughout this day.

Today's Scriptures: Rom. 8:11; Phil. 4:13; Col. 1:11.

June 24

Today God says, *"Let Christ dwell in your heart by faith."*

He promises me: "That Christ may dwell in your hearts by faith; that ye, being rooted and grounded in love, May be able to comprehend with all saints what is the breadth, and length, and depth, and height; And to know the love of Christ, which passeth knowledge" (Eph. 3:17-18).

My response to the Word: These verses are a stunning revelation of what God wants me to experience. He wants me to let Christ dwell in my heart by faith so that I will be rooted and grounded in love — the love of Christ that goes beyond human understanding. This is what I want as well. I will walk in faith and love throughout this day, realizing that, in Christ, the only thing that avails anything is faith which works by love.

My prayer: Lord God, thank you for your amazing love. Let my roots grow deep in the soil of your love, drinking freely from all you have in store for me. I love you, Father; grant that I may know the love of Christ more fully.

Today's Scriptures: Gal. 2:20; Gal. 5:6; Col. 1:27.

June 25

Today God says, *"Be filled with all My fullness."*

He promises me: "And to know the love of Christ, which passeth knowledge, that ye might be filled with all the fulness of God" (Eph. 3:19).

My response to the Word: The thing that impresses me most as I read this verse is the connection between knowing the love of Christ and being filled with all God's fullness. I want both to know Jesus' love fully and to be filled with God's fullness. This is what He wants for me as well. The love of Christ was clearly demonstrated on Calvary. He laid down His life for *me*. After He died and rose again, He ascended into heaven. Then He dispatched His Spirit who seeks to fill me with all God's fullness. I will walk in love and faith this day, completely open to being filled with all the fullness God wants me to have.

My prayer: Father, you are love. Help me to walk in your love throughout this day.

Today's Scriptures: Eph. 5:18; Phil. 1:11; Col. 1:9; 1 John 4:8.

June 26

Today God says, *"I am able to do exceeding abundantly above all that you can ask or think."*

He promises me: "Now unto him that is able to do exceeding abundantly above all that we ask or think, according to the power that worketh in us" (Eph. 3:20).

My response to the Word: God is able to do anything and everything. He knows no limits. Whatever I ask Him for in prayer, He is able to do, if I pray according to His precepts and principles. In fact, He is able to do far more that I even expect. This verse tells me that I have God's power working within me. In context, I know this means God's love and God's Spirit. The more of God's fullness that I have within me assures me that my prayers will be heard and answered.

My prayer: Dear Father, I know you are able to do anything and everything. I express my faith to you. Let your power work within me throughout this day.

Today's Scriptures: Gen. 18:14; 2 Cor. 9:8; Phil. 3:21.

June 27

Today God says, *"Speak the truth in love."*

He promises me: "But speaking the truth in love, may grow up into him in all things, which is the head, even Christ" (Eph. 4:15).

My response to the Word: God wants me to speak the truth at all times, and as I do so to be certain I am communicating with love. Truth and love are key components in my walk with Jesus, and as I practice these qualities I will experience spiritual growth. As I speak the truth in love I will be more like Jesus who was always truthful and loving. I will walk in truth and love throughout this day.

My prayer: Lord, I thank you for empowering me to speak the truth in love. With your help I will do so at all times today.

Today's Scriptures: John 8:32; 2 Cor. 6:7; 2 Tim. 2:15.

June 28

Today God says, *"Be renewed in the spirit of your mind."*

He promises me: "That ye put off concerning the former conversation the old man, which is corrupt according to the deceitful lusts; And be renewed in the spirit of your mind" (Eph. 4:22-23).

My response to the Word: I will cooperate with God in the renewing of my mind by totally detaching from this world system and changing the way I think through the Word of God. The Bible says, ". . . be not conformed to this world: but be ye transformed by the renewing of your mind, that ye may prove what is that good, and acceptable, and perfect, will of God."

My prayer: Father in heaven, I love you and I trust your Word. I want to think like you think; therefore, I ask you to renew my mind through your Word.

Today's Scriptures: Rom. 12:2; 2 Cor. 4:16; Col. 3:10.

June 29

Today God says, *"Walk in love."*

He promises me: "And walk in love, as Christ also hath loved us, and hath given himself for us an offering and a sacrifice to God for a sweetsmelling savour" (Eph. 5:2).

My response to the Word: Throughout this day, with the help of God, I will walk in love, because I know Christ loves me. He demonstrated His great love for me when He died on the cross. "But God commendeth his love toward us, in that, while we were yet sinners, Christ died for us." Through Christ I am able to love others. "We love him, because he first loved us."

My prayer: Help me to walk in your love today, Father. Thank you for demonstrating your love to me through Jesus. In His name I pray.

Today's Scriptures: Rom. 5:8; 1 John 4:8; 1 John 4:19.

June 30

Today God says, *"You are a member of the Body of Christ."*

He promises me: "For we are members of his body, of his flesh, and of his bones" (Eph. 5:30).

My response to the Word: The sacred mystery of actually being a part of Christ goes beyond my ability to understand, but I do know that I am a member of His body, His flesh, and His bones. Paul wrote, "This is a great mystery: but I speak concerning Christ and the church." Christ is the head of the Body; I am a member of the Body. I am miraculously joined to Him and to every other member of the Body. What a privilege; what a blessing!

My prayer: Lord, thank you for letting me be a part of your glorious Body. Help me to be a member that enhances the health and harmony of your entire Body.

Today's Scriptures: 1 Cor. 12:14; 1 Cor. 12:27; Eph. 5:32.

July 1

Today God says, *"Follow Me."*

He promises me: "And be ye kind one to another, tenderhearted, forgiving one another, even as God for Christ's sake hath forgiven you. Be ye therefore followers of God, as dear children" (Eph. 4:32-5:1).

My response to the Word: In order to be a true follower of God, Paul points out, I must learn to "walk in love, as Christ also hath loved us." I will walk in love today as I seek to be a follower of the Lord. Jesus calls me to follow Him, and I deeply desire to walk in His footsteps each moment of the day. Where He leads me I will follow.

My prayer: Heavenly Father, thank you for calling me to the wonderful life in Christ. Lead me, and I will follow you.

Today's Scriptures: Mark 8:34; Luke 5:27; John 21:19; Eph. 5:1-2.

July 2

Today God says, *"Be filled with My Spirit."*

He promises me: "And be not drunk with wine, wherein is excess; but be filled with the Spirit; Speaking to yourselves in psalms and hymns and spiritual songs, singing and making melody in your heart to the Lord" (Eph. 5:18-19).

My response to the Word: I will seek the infilling presence of the Holy Spirit in my life throughout this day. I know God has filled me and He will continue to fill me with His Spirit. It is His Spirit within me that enables me to live victoriously in this present world. I will obey His Word by speaking to myself in psalms and hymns and spiritual songs, singing and making melody in my heart to the Lord.

My prayer: Fill me with your Spirit, Lord, so that I will be able to produce the fruit of your Spirit in all the relationships and responsibilities of my life this day.

Today's Scriptures: Rom. 15:19; 2 Cor. 3:17; 1 John 5:6; Jude 20-21.

July 3

Today God says, *"Give thanks always for all things."*

He promises me: "Giving thanks always for all things unto God and the Father in the name of our Lord Jesus Christ" (Eph. 5:20).

My response to the Word: The attitude of my heart should be one of thankfulness at all times. I am thankful for all God has done for me, what He is doing for me, what He will do for me, and for who He is. He is my Father, and He has given me the name of Jesus Christ, His Son. There is power in the name of Jesus, and I thank my Father for that supernatural source of blessing, victory, and answered prayer.

My prayer: Heavenly Father, thank you for all the blessings I enjoy. I realize you have already blessed me with every spiritual blessing. I thank you for everything you do in the name of Jesus Christ, my Lord.

Today's Scriptures: 1 Cor. 15:57; 2 Cor. 9:15;
Eph. 1:3; 1 Thess. 5:18.

July 4

Today God says, *"Be strong in My power."*

He promises me: "Finally, my brethren, be
strong in the Lord, and in the power of his might"
(Eph. 6:10).

My response to the Word: In order to be
strong in the Lord, and in the power of His might,
I must daily put on the whole armor of God. It
is the armor He provides to me that will protect
me against the devil's schemes. Therefore, I
consciously gird my loins with truth and I put on
the breastplate of righteousness. On my feet, I am
wearing the preparation of the gospel of peace.
The shield of faith enables me to quench all the
fiery darts of the enemy. My head is protected by
the helmet of salvation, and my offensive weapon
is the Word of God — "the sword of the Spirit."

My prayer: Father, thank you for the spiritual
strength you impart to me. I will wear your
protective armor throughout this day, and I
will wield the sword of your Spirit in the warfare
I encounter.

Today's Scriptures: Eph. 6:12-18; 2 Tim. 2:1;
1 John 2:14.

July 5

Today God says, *"To live is Christ; to die is gain."*

He promises me: "For to me to live is Christ, and to die is gain" (Phil. 1:21).

My response to the Word: Jesus has already prepared a place for me in heaven. That's why dying will surely be gain for me. In the meanwhile I will live in the power of Christ that is supplied to me continually through the Holy Spirit, the Word of God, prayer, worship, fellowship, and faith. Throughout this day I will remember that for me to live is Christ, and to die is gain.

My prayer: Loving Lord, your Word shows me that my life is in Christ. He makes my life worthwhile. How I praise Him for giving me abundant life in the here-and-now, and eternal life in the hereafter.

Today's Scriptures: John 1:4; John 10:10; John 14:1-6.

July 6

Today God says, *"I am at work in your life so that My will and purpose will be reflected in your life."*

He promises me, "For it is God which worketh in you both to will and to do of his good pleasure" (Phil. 2:13).

My response to the Word: God is at work in my life at all times. He will not let me down. He continues His workmanship every minute of every day. He wants to conform me to His will so that I can do His good pleasure in every area of my life. I will flow with God throughout this day.

My prayer: Dear Lord, thank you for always being there, and for continuing your workmanship in my life. Help me to conform my life to your will at all times.

Today's Scriptures: Eph. 1:9; Eph. 6:6; Col. 4:12.

July 7

Today God says, *"Let the mind of Jesus Christ be within you."*

He promises me: "Let this mind be in you, which was also in Christ Jesus" (Phil. 2:5).

My response to the Word: Rational thinking may take me to the foot of the mountain, but it is only faith that will take me to the top! Faith comes from the Word of God which represents the mind of Jesus Christ. By letting His Word saturate my heart and mind I allow the mind of Christ to dominate my thoughts.

My prayer: Lord, let the mind of Christ govern my thoughts and words as I go about my daily activities. Span the gap between my thoughts and your thoughts.

Today's Scriptures: 1 Cor. 2:16; 2 Tim. 1:7; Heb. 8:10.

July 8

Today God says, *"The name of Jesus is above every name."*

He promises me: "Wherefore God also hath highly exalted him, and given him a name which is above every name: That at the name of Jesus every knee should bow, of things in heaven, and things in earth, and things under the earth; And that every tongue should confess that Jesus Christ is Lord, to the glory of God the Father" (Phil. 2:9-11).

My response to the Word: The name of Jesus is the most preeminent name in the entire universe. One day every knee will bow at His name, and every tongue will confess that Jesus Christ is Lord. This will bring glory to my Father in heaven. Jesus Christ is my Lord and Savior, and I will proclaim His all-powerful name wherever I go.

My prayer: Heavenly Father, thank you for Jesus Christ, and for the power of His name. When I pray in the name of Jesus demons flee, I experience joy, and my prayers are answered. Thank you, Lord.

July 9

Today God says, *"Be blameless and harmless."*

He promises me: "Do all things without murmurings and disputings: That ye may be blameless and harmless, the sons of God, without rebuke, in the midst of a crooked and perverse nation, among whom ye shine as lights in the world" (Phil. 2:14-15).

My response to the Word: I realize that life itself is a privilege, and my work and ministry are special parts of that privilege. Therefore, I will not complain at all today. I will take care of my responsibilities as a true child of God in the midst of a crooked and perverse nation. With God's help I will shine as a light in the world today.

My prayer: Lord God, thank you for the promises of your Word. Help me to be a light in the darkness throughout this day.

Today's Scriptures: 1 Cor. 1:8; 1 Thess. 5:23; 2 Pet. 3:14.

July 10

Today God says, *"Press toward the mark for the prize of My high calling."*

He promises me: "Forgetting those things which are behind, and reaching forth unto those things which are before, I press toward the mark for the prize of the high calling of God in Christ Jesus" (Phil. 3:13-14).

My response to the Word: God has called me to fulfill His purposes for my life. Therefore, I will press on toward the mark for the prize of His high calling. I choose to forget the negative experiences of the past and to reach for all God has for me. I will live each moment with God, and I know the future will hold good things for me.

My prayer: Lord, thank you for calling me and for enabling me to forget the mistakes of the past. With your help I will reach out for all you have for me.

Today's Scriptures: 1 Cor. 7:20; Eph. 1:18; Eph. 4:4.

July 11

Today God says, *"Rejoice in Me always."*

He promises me: "Rejoice in the Lord alway: and again I say, Rejoice" (Phil. 4:4).

My response to the Word: Throughout this day I will remember that my thankfulness should result from what I have in my heart, not just what I have in my pocket or in the bank. I will rejoice in the Lord always, and I will keep on rejoicing because I realize that He gives me so much for which I am truly thankful. He loves me, saves me, fills me, heals me, prospers me, and blesses me.

My prayer: Lord, I rejoice in you. I praise you, love you, honor you, and adore you. Thank you for being everything to me.

Today's Scriptures: Phil. 3:1; 1 Thess. 5:16; 1 Pet. 1:8.

July 12

Today God says, *"My peace will keep your heart and mind through Christ."*

He promises me: "Be careful for nothing; but in every thing by prayer and supplication with thanksgiving let your requests be made known unto God. And the peace of God, which passeth all understanding, shall keep your hearts and minds through Christ Jesus" (Phil. 4:6-7).

My response to the Word: God gives me peace of mind and peace of heart. Therefore, I will not worry about anything. Instead, I will pray and be thankful. Worry can't change the past, or alter the future, but it certainly can destroy the present moment. I will walk in the peace of God throughout this day.

My prayer: Lord, thank you for your peace which truly does surpass all understanding. By your grace I will enjoy your peace throughout this day.

Today's Scriptures: Heb. 13:20; 1 Pet. 3:11; Jude 2.

July 13

Today God says, *"Set your affection on things above."*

He promises me: "If ye then be risen with Christ, seek those things which are above, where Christ sitteth on the right hand of God. Set your affection on things above, not on things on the earth. For ye are dead, and your life is hid with Christ in God" (Col. 3:1-3).

My response to the Word: I am in Christ and He is in me. I have been raised with Him. Therefore, I will set my mind on heavenly things, not earthly things. I reckon myself to be dead to sin and alive to God through Christ Jesus. Throughout this day I rejoice that my life is safely hid with Christ in God.

My prayer: Heavenly Father, thank you for the power of the Resurrection of Jesus Christ which enables me to keep focused on heavenly things rather than the things of this earth. I praise you, Lord, that death no longer has any sting for me because you have given me the victory through Jesus Christ, my Lord.

Today's Scriptures: Matt. 6:20; John 14:1-6; Rom. 6:11; 1 Cor. 15:55-58.

July 14

Today God says, *"I have delivered you from the power of darkness, and I have translated you into the Kingdom of My dear Son."*

He promises me: "Giving thanks unto the Father, which hath made us meet [able] to be partakers of the inheritance of the saints in light: Who hath delivered us from the power of darkness, and hath translated us into the kingdom of his dear Son" (Col. 1:12-13).

My response to the Word: My heart is filled with gratitude unto my heavenly Father who enabled me to be a partaker of His spiritual inheritance. He has delivered me from the power of darkness and has translated me into the Kingdom of Jesus Christ. Through the blood of Jesus, I have redemption and the forgiveness of my sins.

My prayer: Lord, thank you for preparing me to become a partaker of your inheritance. I know that I have been delivered from the power of darkness. I rejoice over the fact that you have redeemed me and forgiven me, and filled me with the Spirit of your Son, Jesus Christ.

Today's Scriptures: Ps. 32:7; Luke 4:18; Gal. 4:6; Col. 1:14.

July 15

Today God says, *"All things were created by Jesus Christ."*

He promises me: "For by him were all things created, that are in heaven, and that are in earth, visible and invisible, whether they be thrones, or dominions, or principalities, or powers: all things were created by him, and for him" (Col. 1:16).

My response to the Word: Jesus Christ, my Savior and Lord, is "the image of the invisible God, the firstborn of every creature." He created everything that exists in heaven and on earth. Everything was created by Him and for Him. Paul goes on to explain, "He is before all things, and by him all things consist." The Creator of the universe lives in me.

My prayer: Lord God, thank you for Jesus Christ who created all things. I love Him with all my heart.

Today's Scriptures: Col. 1:15; Col. 1:17; Col. 1:27; Rev. 4:11.

July 16

Today God says, *"It pleases Me that all fullness dwells in Jesus Christ."*

He promises me: "For it pleased the Father that in him should all fulness dwell" (Col. 1:19).

My response to the Word: Jesus Christ is before all things, and I want Him to have the preeminence in my life at all times. By Him all things consist — in the universe and in my life as well. He is the center of my life, and He holds everything together for me. He is completion, wholeness, and fullness in every respect. It pleases the Father that all fullness dwells in Jesus. It please me to know that Jesus, who is fullness, lives within me, and I claim His wholeness for my life — spirit, soul, and body.

My prayer: Heavenly Father, thank you for Jesus Christ. I acknowledge the truth that all fullness resides in Him. I will walk in Him, and in His wholeness, throughout this day.

Today's Scriptures: Eph. 1:23; Eph. 3:19; Col. 2:9; 1 Thess. 5:23.

July 17

Today God says, *"All the treasures of wisdom and knowledge are found in Jesus Christ."*

He promises me, "In whom are hid all the treasures of wisdom and knowledge" (Col. 2:3).

My response to the Word: Jesus is my wisdom. In Him I find all the treasures of wisdom and

knowledge. Wisdom is the right use of knowledge. It is knowledge in action. I will apply my
knowledge of God's Word by walking in His
wisdom throughout this day. I realize that my
discovery of God's wisdom and knowledge is one
of the best discoveries I've ever made.

My prayer: Lord, your Word promises me
that you will give me wisdom. I ask for it now, in
faith, nothing wavering. Thank you, Amen.

Today's Scriptures: Ps. 111:10; Prov. 2:6; Prov.
14:33; James 1:5-6.

July 18

Today God says, *"My mercy endures forever."*

He promises me: "O give thanks unto the
Lord; for he is good: because his mercy endureth
for ever. Let Israel now say, that his mercy
endureth for ever" (Ps. 118:1-2).

My response to the Word: My favorite attitude
is gratitude. Truly I have so much to be thankful
for. God's mercies do endure forever, and His
mercies have enabled me to find abundant and
eternal life. Throughout this day I will obey
the Word of God which directs me, "I beseech
you therefore, brethren, by the mercies of God,

that ye present your bodies a living sacrifice, holy,
acceptable unto God, which is your reasonable
service."

My prayer: Heavenly Father, thank you for
the multitude of mercies you've extended to me. I
present my body as a living sacrifice to you
because I know this is my reasonable service of
worship to you.

Today's Scriptures: Prov. 3:3; Matt. 5:7;
Rom. 12:1.

July 19

Today God says, *"There is one Mediator between you
and Me."*

He promises me: "For there is one God, and
one mediator between God and men, the man
Christ Jesus; Who gave himself a ransom for all, to
be testified in due time" (1 Tim. 2:5-6).

My response to the Word: God is my heavenly
Father. My direct access to Him is through Jesus
Christ my Lord. Jesus said, "I am the way, the
truth, and the life: no man cometh unto the
Father, but by me." Because I know this is true,
and because Jesus gave His life as a ransom for
me, I can have confidence that God hears me
when I pray. Blessed be His name.

My prayer: Heavenly Father, thank you for enabling me to have access to your throne-room through Jesus Christ, my Lord. I will remember that He is the sole mediator between you and me.

Today's Scriptures: John 14:6; Heb. 4:16; 1 John 2:1; 1 John 2:2.

July 20

Today God says, *"Faith is the substance of things hoped for and the evidence of things not seen."*

He promises me, "Now faith is the substance of things hoped for, the evidence of things not seen" (Heb. 11:1).

My response to the Word: Faith involves believing what I do not see. Faith pleases God. In one sense, faith is like electricity. Even though I don't often see electricity in action, I can see its evidence manifested in heat and light. The same is true of faith. By the faith that comes from God's Word I believe that Jesus is alive, even though I can't see Him with my physical eyes.

My prayer: Lord, thank you for your Word which builds faith in my heart. I will walk in faith throughout this day.

Today's Scriptures: Rom. 10:17; Col. 1:23; 1 Tim. 6:12; Heb. 11:6; Rev. 1:18.

July 21

Today God says, *"Without faith it is impossible to please Me."*

He promises me, "But without faith it is impossible to please him: for he that cometh to God must believe that he is, and that he is a rewarder of them that diligently seek him" (Heb. 11:6).

My response to the Word: I choose to believe God and His Word because I know this will please Him. I realize that God doesn't call me to be successful; He calls me to be faithful. The literal meaning of "faithful" is "full of faith." I will be a full-of-faith believer throughout this day.

My prayer: Father in heaven, thank you for rewarding my faith. I always want to please you. Continue to build faith in my heart as I meditate upon your Word.

Today's Scriptures: Gal. 2:20; Gal. 3:11; Gal. 5:6.

July 22

Today God says, *"I will not — indeed, cannot — lie to you."*

He promises me, "In hope of eternal life, which God, that cannot lie, promised before the world began" (Titus 1:2).

My response to the Word: I trust God and His Word. His Word is truth. He cannot lie. I will walk in His truth throughout this day. Though truth may not always be popular, I know it is always right. I want to be like God. I never want to lie. I will seek to know truth with my mind and spirit, to accept the truth with my heart, and to let God's truth be enacted in my life.

My prayer: Lord, thank you for your Word which is truth. Your truth has made me free. With your help I will walk in truth throughout this day.

Today's Scriptures: John 8:32; John 17:17; Eph. 4:15; Heb. 10:26.

July 23

Today God says, *"Do not forsake My mercy and truth."*

He promises me: "Let not mercy and truth forsake thee: bind them about thy neck; write them upon the table of thine heart: So shalt thou find favour and good understanding in the sight of God and man" (Prov. 3:3-4).

My response to the Word: I know that God's mercy and truth will never forsake me if I continue to seek them. I will hide God's Word of truth in my heart so that I will not sin against Him. Throughout this day I will remember the Psalmist's words: "Surely goodness and mercy shall follow me all the days of my life: and I will dwell in the house of the Lord for ever".

My prayer: Heavenly Father, help me to bind your mercy and truth to my life and to keep them in my heart. I claim your promise of favor and good understanding in your sight and the sight of men.

Today's Scriptures: Ps. 23:6; Ps. 119:11; Prov. 21:21.

July 24

Today God says, *"In all your ways acknowledge Me, and I will direct your paths."*

He promises me: "Trust in the Lord with all thine heart; and lean not unto thine own understanding. In all thy ways acknowledge him, and he shall direct thy paths" (Prov. 3:5-6).

My response to the Word: I resolve to trust God with all my heart. Throughout this day, therefore, I will not lean upon my own understanding. Rather, I will acknowledge the Lord at all times, and in so doing, I know He will direct my paths. I have surrendered my life to God and I trust Him to love me and guide me.

My prayer: Loving Lord, thank you for your promise to direct my paths. I know you are leading me, and where you lead me I will follow.

Today's Scriptures: Ps. 25:9; Ps. 32:8; Ps. 48:14; 1 John 2:20, 27.

July 25

Today God says, *"Honor Me with your substance."*

He promises me: "Honour the Lord with thy substance, and with the firstfruits of all thine increase: So shall thy barns be filled with plenty, and thy presses shall burst out with new wine" (Prov. 3:9-10).

My response to the Word: God has given so much to me. I am so happy to be able to give it back to Him, and as I do so I realize that He will have further blessings in store for me. Giving is the thermometer of my love. I make a living by what I get, but I make my life by what I give. Throughout this day, therefore, I will take every opportunity to give.

My prayer: Father, you loved the world so much that you gave your only begotten Son. This is love's prerogative — to give and give and give — and this will be my life-style today.

Today's Scriptures: Luke 6:28; 2 Cor. 8-11; Acts 20:35; Eph. 4:28.

July 26

Today God says, *"Depart from evil."*

He promises me: "Be not wise in thine own eyes: fear the Lord, and depart from evil. It shall be health to thy navel, and marrow to thy bones" (Prov. 3:7-8).

My response to the Word: All the wisdom I possess comes from God who has become my wisdom. As I learn to fear Him (with respect and reverence), my wisdom increases. Throughout this day I will seek His wisdom and I will reverentially fear Him. This will lead me to stay far away from evil, and this will give me good health and happiness.

My prayer: Thank you, Lord, for the promise of health you've extended to me if I will seek your wisdom, fear you, and depart from evil. With your help, I will obey you in each of these areas throughout this day.

Today's Scriptures: 1 Thess. 5:22; 1 Tim. 6:10; 2 Tim. 4:18.

July 27

Today God says, *"When I discipline you it is because I love you."*

He promises me: "My son, despise not the chastening of the Lord; neither be weary of his correction: For whom the Lord loveth he correcteth; even as a father the son in whom he delighteth" (Prov. 3:11-12).

My response to the Word: God is my loving heavenly Father. I know that His discipline always results in good things. He loves me, and that is why He corrects me in the same way an earthly father corrects his children because he loves them. Throughout this day I will remember the Lord's discipline in my life, and what He has taught me each time He has lovingly corrected me.

My prayer: Lord God, thank you for your loving discipline in my life. I will respond to it with joy because I know it will help me to grow in you.

Today's Scriptures: Deut. 8:5; Ps. 94:12; Ps. 118:18.

July 28

Today God says, *"My wisdom gives you happiness."*

He promises me: "Happy is the man that findeth wisdom, and the man that getteth understanding. For the merchandise of it is better than the merchandise of silver, and the gain thereof than fine gold" (Prov. 3:13-14).

My response to the Word: God's wisdom in my life gives me great happiness. I find His wisdom in His Word, and understanding His Word brings great happiness to me. Truly, God's wisdom is more valuable to me than gold and silver. Even though an education can be paid for it doesn't necessarily result in wisdom. Wisdom is a gift of God.

My prayer: Lord, you are my wisdom. I receive your wisdom as a gift of your love. Throughout this day I will walk in the wisdom of your Word.

Today's Scriptures: Eph. 1:17; Col. 1:9; Col. 3:16.

July 29

Today God says, *"I will be your confidence."*

He promises me: "Be not afraid of sudden fear, neither of the desolation of the wicked, when it cometh. For the Lord shall be thy confidence, and shall keep thy foot from being taken" (Prov. 3:25-26).

My response to the Word: I've placed my life in the Lord's hands. Therefore, I have no reason to fear anyone or anything. The Lord is my confidence, and I know He will protect me at all times. Today I will walk in the confidence of the Lord. I have complete confidence in the Lord, and I know that no weapon that is formed against me will prosper.

My prayer: Lord, thank you for being my confidence and my strength. Throughout this day I will walk in complete confidence because of you.

Today's Scriptures: Isa. 54:17; Eph. 3:12; Heb. 3:6; 1 John 5:14.

July 30

Today God says, *"My words are life and health to you."*

He promises me: "My son, attend to my words; incline thine ear unto my sayings. Let them not depart from thine eyes; keep them in the midst of thine heart. For they are life unto those that find them, and health to all their flesh" (Prov. 4:20-22).

My response to the Word: God's words are contained in His Word — the Bible. He wants me to keep His words before my eyes and within my heart. I will commit His Word to memory, because I know that the Word of God is life and health for me. My faith in God increases in direct proportion to my knowledge of His Word. I will study God's Word and meditate upon it throughout this day.

My prayer: Lord, thank you for your abiding Word which gives me faith, wisdom, life, and health. I will walk in its light throughout this day.

Today's Scriptures: Ps. 12:6; 2 Tim. 1:13; Rev. 17:17.

July 31

Today God says, *"Keep your heart with all diligence."*

He promises me: "Keep thy heart with all diligence; for out of it are the issues of life" (Prov. 4:23).

My response to the Word: God expects me to keep a watch over my own heart and spirit because this is the place where He resides. His indwelling presence gives me the strength I need to face the challenges of each day. Throughout this day I will endeavor to make sure that the attitudes and thoughts of my heart are in line with His will for me. I will keep my heart with all diligence.

My prayer: Father, help me to keep my heart with all diligence throughout this day. Give me your grace to keep my heart pure.

Today's Scriptures: Ps. 108:1; Ps. 119:2; Prov. 17:22.

August 1

Today God says, *"My commandment is a lamp; My law is a light unto you."*

He promises me: "For the commandment is a lamp; and the law is light; and reproofs of instruction are the way of life" (Prov. 6:23).

My response to the Word: The Psalmist wrote, "Thy word is a lamp unto my feet, and a light unto my path." I believe God's Word, and I will walk in the light it provides throughout this day. His commandments are my lamp and His law (the Bible) is my light, helping me to find my way through this world of darkness. I love God's Word and I will learn its precepts and follow its commandments.

My prayer: Lord, thank you for your Word which truly is a lamp unto my feet and a light unto my path. Help me to walk in the light of your Word throughout this day.

Today's Scriptures: Ps. 119:105; Ps. 119:174; Prov. 3:1.

August 2

Today God says, *"I am understanding, and I have strength."*

He promises me: "Counsel is mine, and sound wisdom: I am understanding; I have strength" (Prov. 8:14).

My response to the Word: The Lord is my wonderful Counselor. I will go to Him with my needs, and I know He will meet each and every one. He provides me with sound wisdom as I need it, and He is my everlasting strength. Throughout this day, therefore, I will not pray to have an easy life; rather, I will pray that I might become a stronger person.

My prayer: Heavenly Father, you are my strength. I will lean upon you today for all the understanding and strength I need.

Today's Scriptures: Isa. 9:6; Eph. 1:18; Eph. 5:17.

August 3

Today God says, *"I am the mighty God."*

He promises me: "For unto us a child is born, unto us a son is given: and the government shall be upon his shoulder: and his name shall be called Wonderful, Counseller, The mighty God, The everlasting Father, The Prince of Peace" (Isa. 9:6).

My response to the Word: Almighty God is my everlasting Father. He is able to do anything and everything in my behalf, including that which seems to be impossible. He is omniscient (all-knowing), omnipotent (all-powerful), and omnipresent (present everywhere). I trust my mighty God with my whole life, realizing that He will supply me with everything I need.

My prayer: Almighty God, thank you for every promise of your Word. I believe you can do everything and anything. You are my everlasting Father.

Today's Scriptures: Gen. 17:1; Gen. 28:3; Phil. 4:19.

August 4

Today God says, *"I am your everlasting Father."*

He promises me: For unto us a child is born, unto us a son is given: and the government shall be upon his shoulder: and his name shall be called Wonderful, Counseller, The mighty God, The everlasting Father, The Prince of Peace" (Isa. 9:6).

My response to the Word: To know that God is my everlasting heavenly Father is the most important information in the world. He will always be there for me. He loves me infinitely more than an earthly father loves his child. My Father makes no mistakes. I realize that my first responsibility to Him is to love Him with all my heart, soul, mind, and strength, and my neighbor as myself

My prayer: Everlasting Father, thank you for loving me with an everlasting love. It is such a privilege to be your child. You are my safe place, Lord.

Today's Scriptures: Gen. 21:33; Ps. 90:2; Prov. 18:10; Hab. 1:12; Luke 10:27.

August 5

Today God says, *"Jesus Christ is the Prince of Peace."*

He promises me: "For unto us a child is born, unto us a son is given: and the government shall be upon his shoulder: and his name shall be called Wonderful, Counseller, The mighty God, The everlasting Father, The Prince of Peace" (Isa. 9:6).

My response to the Word: Jesus gives me supernatural peace. He said, "Peace I leave with you, my peace I give unto you: not as the world giveth, give I unto you. Let not your heart be troubled, neither let it be afraid." Throughout this day I will walk in the peace Jesus gives to me. His peace is a peace that the world cannot give and the world cannot take it away.

My prayer: Lord God, thank you for your gift of peace in my life. Help me to share your peace with everyone I meet today.

Today's Scriptures: John 14:27; 2 Thess. 3:16; Heb. 13:20.

August 6

Today God says, *"I love all those who love Me."*

He promises me: "I love them that love me; and those that seek me early shall find me" (Prov. 8:17).

My response to the Word: I love the Lord, and I know He loves me. His lovingkindness is better than life to me. I will walk in the knowledge of His love throughout this day. The sunlight of God's love will kill all the germs of jealousy, hate, and sin in my life.

My prayer: Thank you for loving me, Father. I want to learn how to love you with all my heart, mind, soul, and strength.

Today's Scriptures: Ps. 63:3; Matt. 22:37-39; John 3:16.

August 7

Today God says, *"Those who seek Me early will find Me."*

He promises me, "I love them that love me; and those that seek me early shall find me" (Prov. 8:17).

My response to the Word: At the beginning of each day I will seek the Lord, and throughout this day I will obey Jesus who said, "But seek first the kingdom of God, and his righteousness; and all these things shall be added unto you." I will put God and His Word first in my life all day long.

My prayer: Heavenly Father, thank you for your promise which declares that I will find you if I will seek you early. Draw me to you throughout this day.

Today's Scriptures: Matt. 6:33; Matt. 7:7; Acts 17:27.

August 8

Today God says, *"I will lead you in the way of righteousness."*

He promises me: "I lead in the way of righteousness, in the midst of the paths of judgment" (Prov. 8:20).

My response to the Word: God is leading me in His paths, because He is my Shepherd. The Psalmist wrote, "The Lord is my shepherd; I shall not want. He maketh me to lie down in green pastures: he leadeth me beside the still waters. He restoreth my soul: he leadeth me in the paths of righteousness for his name's sake." He leads me — what a blessed thought!

My prayer: Heavenly Father, continue to lead me in the paths of your righteousness throughout this day. Thank you for restoring my soul.

Today's Scriptures: Ps. 5:8; Ps. 7:8; Ps. 23:1-3.

August 9

Today God says, *"Seek Me, and you shall live."*

He promises me: "For thus saith the Lord unto the house of Israel, Seek ye me, and ye shall live" (Amos 5:4).

My response to the Word: Before I knew the Lord I wasn't truly alive. When He called me out of the world, I walked into a whole new life. Christianity truly is the land of new beginnings, and each new day is a new adventure with Christ. He has given me newness of life, abundant life, and eternal life. He is life to me.

My prayer: Lord, thank you for the gift of life. As I seek you today I know you will bless me with newness of life. I will walk in newness of life throughout this day.

Today's Scriptures: Deut. 4:29; 1 Chron. 16:11; Ps. 91:15-16.

August 10

Today God says, *"Let My Word dwell in you richly."*

He promises me: "Let the word of Christ dwell in you richly in all wisdom" (Col. 3:16).

My response to the Word: The Word of God is the greatest resource I have on this earth. It reveals the Father's will to me. I will pray the Word, meditate upon it, let its truths soak into my spirit, walk according to its principles, memorize its verses, and keep it hidden in my heart. The result will be victory, power, strength, cleansing, renewal, trust, faith, and hope. I will walk in God's Word today as I let it dwell in me richly.

My prayer: Father, thank you for your Word which dwells in me richly in all wisdom. I will let its riches and wisdom be a great treasure in my life.

Today's Scriptures: Ps. 107:20; Isa. 40:8; John 1:1.

August 11

Today God says, *"Do everything in the name of the Lord Jesus."*

He promises me: "And whatsoever ye do in word or deed, do all in the name of the Lord Jesus, giving thanks to God and the Father by him" (Col. 3:17).

My response to the Word: As I go about my daily activities this day I will remember to do everything in the name of the Lord Jesus. I will cultivate this approach to life by being thankful at all times, remembering the admonition of the Great Apostle: "In every thing give thanks: for this is the will of God in Christ Jesus concerning you."

My prayer: Dear Lord, I love you with all my heart. Help me to do everything today in the name of the Lord Jesus, with a thankful heart.

Today's Scriptures: 1 Thess. 5:18; Rev. 15:4; Rev. 19:13.

August 12

Today God says, *"In the way of righteousness there is life."*

He promises me: "In the way of righteousness is life; and in the pathway thereof there is no death" (Prov. 12:28).

My response to the Word: The Bible is replete with admonitions about the importance of righteousness. Though I realize I have no righteousness of my own, I am able to walk in the righteousness that Christ has imparted to me. The Bible says, "The righteous is delivered out of trouble," and "The righteousness of the perfect shall direct his way." I will walk in the Lord's righteousness throughout this day.

My prayer: Lord, thank you for imparting your righteousness to me. With your help I will walk in righteousness everywhere I go.

Today's Scriptures: Ps. 23:3; Prov. 11:5; Prov. 11:8.

August 13
_____

Today God says, *"I give My favor to you."*

He promises me: "A good man obtaineth favour of the Lord: but a man of wicked devices will he condemn" (Prov. 12:2).

My response to the Word: I will walk in the goodness of God throughout this day. The Lord gives His wonderful favor to those who walk in goodness. I will remember that the best way to escape evil is to pursue good and that goodness consists not so much in the outward things I do, but in the inward attitudes of my heart.

My prayer: God, my loving Father, thank you for your goodness. Fill me with your Spirit so that I will be enabled to walk in goodness throughout this day.

Today's Scriptures: Ps. 5:12; Prov. 3:4; Prov. 8:35.

August 14

Today God says, *"Keep a watch over your mouth."*

He promises me: "He that keepeth his mouth keepeth his life: but he that openeth wide his lips shall have destruction" (Prov. 13:3).

My response to the Word: With God's help I will be able to control my speech. I will keep a watch over the way I use my words this day. Someone once wisely observed, "If God had intended that we should talk more than we hear, He would have given us two mouths and one ear." I will listen more, and speak less throughout this day.

My prayer: Father, thank you for the gift of speech. Help me to bridle my tongue, and set a watch before my lips.

Today's Scriptures: Prov. 18:21; Rom. 10:8; James 3.

August 15

Today God says, *"In a multitude of words sin can usually be found."*

·   *He promises me:* "In the multitude of words there wanteth not sin: but he that refraineth his lips is wise" (Prov. 10:19).

My response to the Word: It is so important to choose my words carefully before I speak. This I will do throughout this day, with God's help. Even when I am saying something that is worthwhile today I will try to do so with as few words as possible. Sometimes a multiplicity of words indicates a lack of thought.

My prayer: Help me, Lord, to choose my words carefully. Keep me from using my speech in a careless way.

Today's Scriptures: Ps. 81:10; Matt. 12:34; Rom. 10:9.

August 16

Today God says, *"Commit your works to Me, and I will establish your thoughts."*

He promises me: "Commit thy works unto the Lord, and thy thoughts shall be established" (Prov. 16:3).

My response to the Word: Throughout this day I will keep my mind focused on God and I will commit everything I do unto Him. In this way I know my mind will be renewed and my thoughts will be established. Acting (or speaking) without thinking is a lot like shooting without aiming. My goal is to think God's thoughts (as they are expressed in His Word) throughout this day.

My prayer: Lord, I commit my works to you. Thank you for establishing my thoughts.

Today's Scriptures: Ps. 31:5; Ps. 37:5; 2 Tim. 1:12.

August 17

Today God says, *"I have made all things for myself."*

He promises me: "The Lord hath made all things for himself: yea, even the wicked for the day of evil" (Prov. 16:4).

My response to the Word: God is the Creator of the entire universe. He is my Creator, and I realize that He created me in His own image. He created me to worship Him and enjoy Him forever. Throughout this day, therefore, I will remember that God made me for himself. I give my life to Him afresh.

My prayer: Lord, thank you for creating me in just the way you did. It gives me great pleasure to serve you, and I will worship you forever.

Today's Scriptures: Gen. 1:27; Col. 1:16; Rev. 4:11.

August 18

Today God says, *"When you please Me I will make your enemies to be at peace with you."*

He promises me: "When a man's ways please the Lord, he maketh even his enemies to be at peace with him" (Prov. 16:7).

My response to the Word: Above all else, I want to please the Lord today. I will seek to please Him with every thought, word, and deed. I know that without faith it is impossible to please God. Therefore, I will obey God's Word which teaches me to walk in love and live by faith. I will seek first the Kingdom of God and His righteousness. I will build my life upon the rock of God's Word.

My prayer: Father God, I love you. Help me to be pleasing to you and make my enemies be at peace with me.

Today's Scriptures: Matt. 6:33; Matt. 7:24; Gal. 3:11; Eph. 5:2; Heb. 11:6.

August 19

Today God says, *"When you do good deeds in secret I will reward you."*

He promises me: "But when thou doest alms, let not thy left hand know what thy right hand doeth: That thine alms may be in secret: and thy Father which seeth in secret himself shall reward thee openly" (Matt. 6:3-4).

My response to the Word: Goodness does not necessarily consist in the outward things I do, but in the inward things I am. I want to walk in honesty, openness, and integrity throughout this day. I will take every opportunity to give and to do good to others. As I do so, I will remember that God is watching me, and this knowledge alone is a great reward.

My prayer: Father, thank you for watching over me. I am greatly blessed by your promise to reward me.

Today's Scriptures: 1 Cor. 15:58; Gal. 6:9; 2 Thess. 3:13.

August 20

Today God says, *"The Kingdom of heaven belongs to the poor in spirit."*

He promises me: "Blessed are the poor in spirit: for theirs is the kingdom of heaven" (Matt. 5:3).

My response to the Word: Blessedness is the blissful state of being blessed so much that happiness automatically results. I am blessed by my loving Father, as I become aware that I am completely dependent upon Him (poor in spirit). He enables me to see myself as I really am — a person who needs God. Throughout this day I will remember that as I acknowledge my dependence upon God, He shares the blessings of His Kingdom with me.

My prayer: Dear Lord, thank you for blessing me so much. I depend on you and I am blessed. I praise your holy name!

Today's Scriptures: Luke 6:20; John 15:5; James 2:5.

August 21

Today God says, *"I will comfort you when you mourn."*

He promises me: "Blessed are they that mourn: for they shall be comforted" (Matt. 5:4).

My response to the Word: Whenever I have experienced loss in my life, God has always been there to give me His comfort. In fact, I know Him to be "the God of all comfort." God promises me that He will both comfort me and bless me in any time of mourning that I will have to face. I believe Him and trust Him to fulfill His promise to me.

My prayer: Lord, thank you for being "the God of all comfort." I will walk in the knowledge of your comfort throughout this day.

Today's Scriptures: Ps. 23; Isa. 66:13; 2 Cor. 1:3.

August 22

Today God says, *"Your hunger for righteousness will be satisfied."*

He promises me: "Blessed are they which do hunger and thirst after righteousness: for they shall be filled" (Matt. 5:6).

My response to the Word: There is great happiness and blessedness in the knowledge that God will fill me with His righteousness in fulfillment of my spiritual hunger and thirst. His Word proclaims: "But seek ye first the kingdom of God, and his righteousness; and all these things shall be added unto you."

My prayer: Father, thank you for your promise to fill me when I seek after your righteousness. Thank you for quenching my thirst and satisfying my hunger.

Today's Scriptures: Matt. 6:33; John 4:13; John 6:35.

August 23

Today God says, *"Be merciful, and you shall receive mercy."*

He promises me: "Blessed are the merciful: for they shall obtain mercy" (Matt. 5:7).

My response to the Word: God's mercy and faithfulness are new to me each day. I will walk in

His mercy and share His mercy wherever I go today. God's mercy and grace stem from His great compassion for me. Though I do not deserve these blessings, I receive them and determine to show my gratitude for them at all times by extending mercy and compassion to those around me.

My prayer: Heavenly Father, thank you for your mercy, grace, and favor in my life. I will walk in your mercy throughout this day.

Today's Scriptures: Ps. 107; Jer. 33:11; Dan. 9:4.

August 24

Today God says, *"Keep your heart pure, and you will see Me."*

He promises me: "Blessed are the pure in heart: for they shall see God" (Matt. 5:8).

My response to the Word: Throughout this day I will seek purity of heart. I will keep my head and my heart going in the right direction, and then I will not have to worry about my feet. I realize that happiness, as Jesus pointed out, consists of a healthy mental attitude, a grateful spirit, a clear conscience, and a pure heart. I will strive to maintain all four of these attributes throughout this day. When I fall short of the mark, I will plead the merits of the blood of Christ which cleanses me.

My prayer: Lord, thank you for making it possible for me to have heart-purity. I will walk in purity of heart today, realizing that one day I will be with you.

Today's Scriptures: Ps. 12:6; Prov. 30:5; Titus 1:15; 1 John 1:7.

August 25

Today God says, *"I want you to be a peacemaker."*

He promises me: "Blessed are the peacemakers: for they shall be called the children of God" (Matt. 5:9).

My response to the Word: Peace comes from knowing Jesus Christ. In fact, He is my peace. He has called me to peace. Through Jesus Christ I know true peace which I am able to share with others. God says that the fruit of righteousness is sown by those who are peacemakers. As God's child I will endeavor to be a peacemaker.

My prayer: Lord, thank you for perfect peace that takes away all worry and fear. With your help and your wisdom I will walk in your peace and be a peacemaker throughout this day.

Today's Scriptures: John 14:27; 1 Cor. 7:15; Eph. 2:14; James 3:17-18.

August 26

Today God says, *"Keep My commandments, and I will love you."*

He promises me: "He that hath my commandments and keepeth them, he it is that loveth me: and he that loveth me shall be loved of my Father, and I will love him, and will manifest myself to him" (John 14:21).

My response to the Word: God gives me His commandments because He loves me. The commandments are not in place in order to make my life more difficult or unpleasant, but they serve to protect me and lead me into happiness. With the help of His Spirit, I will obey God at all times. I realize that delayed obedience is the brother of disobedience, so I will be sure to take every opportunity to obey this day.

My prayer: Lord, lead me and empower me so that I will keep your commandments at all times. Thank you for loving me, being with me and manifesting yourself to me.

Today's Scriptures: John 15:12; 1 John 2:7; 2 John 6.

August 27

Today God says, *"You are My friend if you do whatever I command you to do."*

He promises me: "Ye are my friends, if ye do whatsoever I command you" (John 15:14).

My response to the Word: It stuns me to think that God wants to be my friend. I realize that friendship with God is a relationship that entails a deeper commitment and greater responsibility than most friendships. Jesus said, "Henceforth I call you not servants; for the servant knoweth not what his lord doeth: but I have called you friends; for all things that I have heard of my Father I have made known unto you."

My prayer: Lord, thank you for calling me to be your friend. I want always to walk with you, in close friendship with you.

Today's Scriptures: Prov. 17:17; John 15:14; John 15:15.

August 28

Today God says, "*I have given you victory.*"

He promises me: "But thanks be to God, which giveth us the victory through our Lord Jesus Christ" (1 Cor. 15:57).

My response to the Word: God wants me to be a winner. In fact, He has already given me the victory over every weakness and problem through Jesus Christ, my Lord. Because of Him, I am completely victorious over sin, death, fear, and every other enemy. I will walk in the victory God has given to me throughout this day.

My prayer: Lord, thank you for victory. I am more than a conqueror through you.

Today's Scriptures: Rom. 8:37; 1 Cor. 15:54; 1 John 5:4.

August 29

Today God says, *"I am the Father of mercies."*

He promises me: "Blessed be God, even the Father of our Lord Jesus Christ, the Father of mercies, and the God of all comfort" (2 Cor. 1:3).

My response to the Word: My Father is the Father of my Lord Jesus Christ, and He is the Father of mercies. He is also the God of all comfort in my life. I bless the Lord for His mercies and comfort in my life. I respond to His mercy by giving all that I am and hope to be to Him.

My prayer: Father of mercies and God of all comfort, I give myself to you. Thank you for your mercy and comfort in my life.

Today's Scriptures: Lam. 3:22; Rom. 12:1; Col. 3:12.

August 30

Today God says, "*I will comfort you during times of tribulation.*"

He promises me: "Who comforteth us in all our tribulation, that we may be able to comfort them which are in any trouble, by the comfort wherewith we ourselves are comforted of God" (2 Cor. 1:4).

My response to the Word: God always gives me comfort when I am going through times of loss, tribulation, and trouble. I know He loves me. I receive His comforting presence even now. As I meet people today who are in any kind of trouble I will comfort them with the same comfort I have received from God.

My prayer: Loving Lord, thank you for always being there for me. Enable me to comfort those in any kind of trouble with your comfort and compassion.

Today's Scriptures: Isa. 51:3; Acts 9:31; Rom. 15:4.

August 31

Today God says, "*All of My promises are yes and amen.*"

He promises me: "For all the promises of God in him are yea, and in him Amen, unto the glory of God by us" (2 Cor. 1:20).

My response to the Word: God is the great Promise-keeper, and He wants me to be a promise-reaper in His kingdom. Every word of the Bible is true, and it is ". . . given by inspiration of God, and is profitable for doctrine, for reproof, for correction, for instruction in righteousness: That the man of God may be throughly furnished unto all good works." Is a particular promise for me? In Christ the answer is yes and amen. Every promise in the Bible is mine.

My prayer: Thank you, Lord, for all the wonderful promises of your Word. I believe your Word, and I know your promises are for *me*.

Today's Scriptures: 2 Tim. 3:16; Heb. 11:33; 2 Pet. 1:4.

September 1

Today God says, *"I have not given you a spirit of fear."*

He promises me: "For God hath not given us the spirit of fear; but of power, and of love, and of a sound mind" (2 Tim. 1:7).

My response to the Word: When fear sails into the sea of my mind, I will remember that faith is there too, and I will permit only faith to lay anchor in my mind. God has given me the spirit of power, love, and a sound mind. The Lord wants me to walk in His power, love, and sound mind throughout this day, and with His help, I will do so.

My prayer: Dear Father, thank you for removing fear from my life, and for replacing it with your love, power, and soundness of mind. I will walk in your ways today.

Today's Scriptures: Acts 3:16; Acts 9:34; 1 Thess. 5:23.

September 2

Today God says, *"I have inspired My Word so that you will be furnished for all good works."*

He promises me: "All scripture is given by inspiration of God, and is profitable for doctrine, for reproof, for correction, for instruction in righteousness: That the man of God may be perfect, throughly furnished unto all good works" (2 Tim. 3:16-17).

My response to the Word: The Bible is the foundation of my life. It is inspired by God so that I might grow spiritually. God is perfecting me through His Word so that I might be better prepared to do good works for Him. The Bible is a book of prayers, answers, and promises. I will walk in the light of God's Word throughout this day.

My prayer: Lord, thank you for your Word and for the doctrine, reproof, correction, and instruction in righteousness it provides for me. Help me to walk in your Word today.

Today's Scriptures: 2 Tim. 2:15; Titus 1:9; Heb. 4:12.

September 3

Today God says, *"I have called you with a holy calling."*

He promises me: "Who hath saved us, and called us with an holy calling, not according to our works, but according to his own purpose and grace, which was given us in Christ Jesus before the world began" (2 Tim. 1:9).

My response to the Word: God has saved me and He has called me with a holy calling through His grace. "For by grace are ye saved through faith; and that not of yourselves: it is the gift of God: Not of works, lest any man should boast." God's marvelous grace has reached me in my moment of deepest need. He has saved me and called me with a holy calling. Praise His name!

My prayer: Father, thank you for saving me and calling me by your grace. I will always live for you.

Today's Scriptures: Rom. 11:29; Eph. 1:18; Eph. 2:8-9; Phil. 3:14.

September 4

Today God says, *"The blood of Jesus has redeemed you and given you forgiveness of your sins."*

He promises me: "In whom we have redemption through his blood, the forgiveness of sins, according to the riches of his grace" (Eph. 1:7).

My response to the Word: Through the blood of Jesus I have redemption and forgiveness. The blood of Jesus Christ cleanses me of all my sin. The Bible says, "If we confess our sins, he is faithful and just to forgive us our sins, and to cleanse us from all unrighteousness."

My prayer: Lord, thank you for the blood of Jesus Christ which cleanses me from all my sins. I will walk in His forgiveness throughout this day.

Today's Scriptures: 1 John 1:7; 1 John 1:9; Rev. 1:5.

September 5

Today God says, *"My Word will help you grow."*

He promises me: "As newborn babes, desire the sincere milk of the word, that ye may grow thereby" (1 Pet. 2:2).

My response to the Word: I desire the sweet milk of God's Word because I know it will help me to grow spiritually. God's Word is more powerful than any two-edged sword: "For the word of God is quick, and powerful, and sharper than any two-edged sword, piercing even to the dividing asunder of soul and spirit, and of the joints and marrow, and is a discerner of the thoughts and intents of the heart."

My prayer: Dear Lord, thank you for your Word which is the sword of the Spirit. The power of your Word will nourish me and help me grow spiritually throughout this day.

Today's Scriptures: Eph. 6:17; Heb. 4:12; 1 Pet. 1:23.

September 6

Today God says, *"My name is a strong tower in which you can find refuge."*

He promises me: "The name of the Lord is a strong tower: the righteous runneth into it, and is safe" (Prov. 18:10).

My response to the Word: The wonderful names of the Lord God tell me who He really is to

me. He is Jehovah-Jireh, my Provider. He is
Jehovah-Shammah, the God who is always there.
He is Jehovah-Ro'eh, my Shepherd. He is Yahweh,
the God who never changes. He is Adonai, the
eternal Lord. He is Jehovah-Repheka, my Healer,
and Jehovah-Elyon, the Lord God most high, and
Jehovah-Tsidkenu, the Righteous Lord. Knowing
these names of my wonderful Lord reveals who
He is to me.

My prayer: Lord God, thank you for your
names which reveal your unchanging character to
me. In your names I find great refuge.

Today's Scriptures: Acts 2:21; Eph. 1:21;
Phil. 2:8-11.

September 7

Today God says, *"I am your Friend; I am closer to
you than a brother."*

He promises me: "A man that hath friends
must shew himself friendly: and there is a friend
that sticketh closer than a brother" (Prov. 18:24).

My response to the Word: God is my personal
friend, and throughout this day I will seek to
develop an intimate relationship with Him. He
truly does stick closer than a brother to me. He is
the greater One who lives in me. Friendships will
last when they are cultivated and nurtured with

a lot of careful attention, and I will always endeavor to cultivate a close personal relationship with my Lord.

My prayer: Thank you, Father, for loving me. Thank you for wanting to be my friend. I will walk in the comfort of your friendship throughout this day.

Today's Scriptures: John 15:13-14; James 4:4; 1 John 4:4.

September 8

Today God says, *"I will keep you safe."*

He promises me: "The horse is prepared against the day of battle: but safety is of the Lord" (Prov. 21:31).

My response to the Word: God is my place of refuge; He is my safety. I will walk in the safety He provides throughout this day. Safety is protection from harm, and God is my Protector. In fact, He promises me, "Yea, though I walk through the valley of the shadow of death, I will fear no evil: for thou art with me: thy rod and thy staff they comfort me."

My prayer: Lord, thank you for being my Shepherd who protects me, feeds me, guides me, and keeps me safe. I put my life in your hands, realizing that you always take good care of your children.

Today's Scriptures: Ps. 23:4; Ps. 62:7; Ps. 142:5.

September 9

Today God says, *"My law is perfect, and it will restore your soul."*

He promises me: "The law of the Lord is perfect, converting [restoring] the soul: the testimony of the Lord is sure, making wise the simple" (Ps. 19:7).

My response to the Word: God's law and His testimonies are fully revealed in His Word. I will walk in the light of His Word throughout this day, claiming His promises of wholeness, spiritual restoration, and wisdom. I know that the knowledge, understanding, and appropriation of the Word of God are my means of spiritual growth.

My prayer: Thank you, Lord, for your Word which gives me hope, stability, faith, and purpose in my daily life. Strengthen me through your Word.

Today's Scriptures: Ps. 51:12; Ps. 119:28; Jer. 30:17; Matt. 17:11.

September 10

Today God says, *"My Word gives you joy and enlightenment."*

He promises me: "The statutes of the Lord are right, rejoicing the heart: the commandment of the Lord is pure, enlightening the eyes" (Ps. 19:8).

My response to the Word: I find God's commandments and His statutes in His Word. As I discover the various principles and precepts of His Word I find joy and enlightenment. God's Word brings light to my soul. I rejoice because my spirit is the candle of the Lord. The entrance of His Word gives me understanding. The mercies and salvation of the Lord come unto me according to His Word.

My prayer: Lord God, thank you for your Word which truly does give me joy and enlightenment. Quicken me today according to your Word.

Today's Scriptures: Ps. 119:25, 41, 130, 169; Prov. 20:27; 1 Pet. 1:8; 1 John 1:4.

September 11

Today God says, *"When you keep My commandments, I will reward you."*

He promises me: "More to be desired are they than gold, yea, than much fine gold: sweeter also than honey and the honeycomb. Moreover by them is thy servant warned: and in keeping of them there is great reward" (Ps. 19:10-11).

My response to the Word: I desire the truth of God's Word more than anything else because I know it is more valuable than fine gold and it is sweeter than honey. Through the Word of God, the Lord teaches me, and He also promises to reward me when I am obedient. I will walk in obedience to the Word of God throughout this day.

My prayer: Lord, thank you for your Word. Help me to obey it at all times.

Today's Scriptures: Ps. 1:2; Ps. 19:7; Ps. 119:174.

September 12

Today God says, *"I will hear you in times of trouble."*

He promises me: "The Lord hear thee in the day of trouble: the name of the God of Jacob defend thee" (Ps. 20:1).

My response to the Word: In times of trouble I know the Lord will hear me when I call to Him. He promises to help me and to defend me. Therefore, I know that no matter what may come my way, God will be there to protect me. It is when I think I can handle my difficulties without God that I get into trouble.

My prayer: Lord, thank you for being my refuge in times of trouble. Thank you for hearing and answering my prayers.

Today's Scriptures: Ps. 4:3; Ps. 5:3; Ps. 8:9; 1 John 5:15.

September 13

Today God says, *"I am your Shepherd."*

He promises me: "The Lord is my shepherd; I shall not want. He maketh me to lie down in green pastures: he leadeth me beside the still waters" (Ps. 23:1-2).

My response to the Word: A shepherd is one who guides, guards, nurtures, and protects his sheep. I am happy to be a sheep who is in the care of the Good Shepherd. The Lord is my Shepherd, and He is so committed to me that He laid down His life for me. Jesus said, "I am the good shepherd: the good shepherd giveth his life for the sheep"

My prayer: Lord, thank you for being my Shepherd. Because of your constant care in my life, I know all my needs will be met.

Today's Scriptures: John 10:11; John 10:14; John 10:16; 1 Pet. 2:25.

September 14

Today God says, *"Goodness and mercy will always follow you."*

He promises me: "Surely goodness and mercy shall follow me all the days of my life: and I will dwell in the house of the Lord for ever" (Ps. 23:6).

My response to the Word: Goodness and mercy, like two coachman on the back of a royal coach, will always be with me, and I will dwell in the house of the Lord forever. What a promise this is — goodness and mercy in the here-and-now, and life in God's house in the hereafter. I will walk in the certainty of this promise throughout this day.

My prayer: God, I thank you for your goodness and mercy which are with me constantly. I will recognize that they are part of my life throughout this day.

Today's Scriptures: Ps. 52:1; Ps. 107:1; Rom. 15:14.

September 15

Today God says, *"I am the God of patience and consolation."*

He promises me: "Now the God of patience and consolation grant you to be like-minded one toward another according to Christ Jesus" (Rom. 15:5).

My response to the Word: God is the God of patience and consolation, and He wants me to be like-minded toward other believers in the way Christ outlined. Patience comes from my heavenly Father, and so does consolation — a strong form of comfort. Through the power of God I will walk in patience throughout this day, because I know it will strengthen my spirit, sweeten my disposition, stifle my anger, subdue my pride, and bridle my tongue.

My prayer: Thank you, Father, for the patience and comfort that your Word gives to me through your Spirit. Help me to walk in patience all day long.

Today's Scriptures: John 17; Phil. 2:1; 2 Thess. 2:16.

September 16

Today God says, *"My Kingdom consists of righteousness, peace, and joy in the Holy Spirit."*

He promises me: "For the kingdom of God is not meat and drink; but righteousness, and peace, and joy in the Holy Ghost" (Rom. 14:17).

My response to the Word: God has translated me into the Kingdom of His dear Son. I believe God's Word, and I claim its promise of righteousness, peace, and joy through the Holy Spirit as my inheritance as a child of God. God's Kingdom is found wherever the King of kings rules. He sits on His throne in heaven, and also on His throne within my heart. This fact enables me to appropriate His righteousness, peace, and joy for this day.

My prayer: Father, I thank you for your kingdom in which I find righteousness, peace, and joy. Fill me with your Spirit as I walk in your righteousness, peace, and joy today.

Today's Scriptures: Luke 17:21; John 18:36; 1 Cor. 4:20; Col. 1:13.

September 17

Today God says, *"I will have mercy upon you if you will forsake and confess your sins."*

He promises me: "He that covereth his sins shall not prosper: but whoso confesseth and forsaketh them shall have mercy" (Prov. 28:13).

My response to the Word: God grants repentance to my heart when I sin. Repentance means both to be sorry for my sins and to turn away from them. God promises to give His mercy to me when I confess and forsake my sins; therefore, I will confess, forsake, and turn away from my sins as soon as the Holy Spirit convicts me.

My prayer: Lord, I never want to attempt to cover my sins again. Instead, I want to forsake them and follow you. Grant me your gift of repentance when I sin.

Today's Scriptures: Rom. 10:9; James 5:16; 2 John 7.

September 18

Today God says, *"Walk in faithfulness, and you will abound with blessings."*

He promises me: "A faithful man shall abound with blessings: but he that maketh haste to be rich shall not be innocent" (Prov. 28:20).

My response to the Word: The word "faithful" literally means to be full of faith. A faithful person is so full of faith that he or she is steady in his or her commitments to God, self, and others. Faithfulness is a fruit of the Spirit: "But the fruit of the Spirit is love, joy, peace, longsuffering, gentleness, goodness, faith, Meekness, temperance: against such there is no law."

My prayer: Heavenly Father, thank you for being faithful to me. I want to be faithful to you. Help me to walk in faithfulness throughout this day.

Today's Scriptures: Ps. 89:1; Lam. 3:23; Gal. 5:22-23.

September 19

Today God says, *"Do not let evil overcome you; instead, overcome evil with good."*

He promises me: "Be not overcome of evil, but overcome evil with good" (Rom. 12:21).

My response to the Word: God gives me the power to overcome evil with good so that I can obey His admonition: "Therefore if thine enemy hunger, feed him; if he thirst, give him drink: for in so doing thou shalt heap coals of fire on his head." Throughout this day I want to respond to my tormentors, accusers, persecutors, and enemies in the way Christ teaches — loving them, blessing them, doing good to them and praying for them.

My prayer: Lord, thank you for showing me how I should respond when others come against me in any form. Empower me to respond with goodness when others are evil toward me.

Today's Scriptures: Matt. 5:44; Rom. 12:20; Eph. 4:32.

September 20

Today God says, *"All My words are pure."*

He promises me: "Every word of God is pure: he is a shield unto them that put their trust in him" (Prov. 30:5).

My response to the Word: God's Word is pure truth. It reveals to me that God is my shield. The Bible says, "As for God, his way is perfect: the word of the Lord is tried: he is a buckler to all those that trust in him." I believe that God is my shield. I know that His Word has been proven to be true. Therefore, I will walk in the pure light of His Word throughout this day.

My prayer: Lord, I love your Word. Thank you for the purity it brings into my heart and life. I will walk in its purity throughout this day.

Today's Scriptures: Ps. 18:30; Ps. 119:140; Heb. 4:12.

September 21

Today God says, *"I am your Rock."*

He promises me: "The God of my rock; in him will I trust: he is my shield, and the horn of my salvation, my high tower, and my refuge, my saviour; thou savest me from violence. I will call on the Lord, who is worthy to be praised: so shall I be saved from mine enemies" (2 Sam. 22:3-4).

My response to the Word: God is my Rock, the solid foundation on which I take my stand and build my life. I trust Him to watch out for me at all times, because I know He is my shield, my refuge, and my Savior. He promises to save me from violence and all my enemies. I will walk in the security of this promise throughout this day.

My prayer: Lord, thank you for being the solid foundation of my life. I believe your promises to me.

Today's Scriptures: Ps. 18:2; Ps. 18:46; Ps. 62:2.

September 22

Today God says, *"I hear your cries."*

He promises me: "In my distress I called upon the Lord, and cried to my God: and he did hear my voice out of his temple, and my cry did enter into his ears" (2 Sam. 22:7).

My response to the Word: In times of trouble and difficulty, I will cry to the Lord, remembering that He is only a prayer away. I know He hears my cries to Him. The Prophet Jeremiah wrote, "Call unto me, and I will answer thee, and shew thee great and mighty things, which thou knowest not." I believe God.

My prayer: Lord, thank you for always being there to hear my cries and answer my prayers. I love you with all my heart.

Today's Scriptures: Jer. 33:3; Dan. 9:17-19; 1 John 5:15.

September 23

Today God says, *"I will heal you."*

He promises me: "Thus saith the Lord, the God of David thy father, I have heard thy prayer, I have seen thy tears: behold, I will heal thee" (2 Kings 20:5).

My response to the Word: God hears my prayers and He sees my tears. He promises to heal me. Isaiah, the prophet, declared: "But he was wounded for our transgressions, he was bruised for our iniquities: the chastisement of our peace was upon him; and with his stripes we are healed." God is my Healer, and I claim His promise of healing and health for me and my entire family.

My prayer: Lord, thank you for your promise of healing. I will walk in the health you give to me throughout this day.

Today's Scriptures: Isa. 53:5; Mal. 4:2; Acts 10:38.

September 24

Today God says, *"I have delivered you from all your fears."*

He promises me: "I sought the Lord, and he heard me, and delivered me from all my fears" (Ps. 34:4).

My response to the Word: I will seek God. When I pray to Him, I know He hears me. Through prayer and His perfect love I will be delivered from all my fears. Prayer is the prelude to peace, the prologue to power, the preface to purpose, and the pathway to perfection. I will pray without ceasing today.

My prayer: Lord, thank you for the power of prayer. Help me to practice your presence through prayer throughout this day.

Today's Scriptures: 1 Thess. 5:18; 2 Tim. 3:11; 2 Tim. 4:17; James 5:16.

September 25

Today God says, *"Call upon Me in times of trouble, and I will deliver you."*

He promises me: "Offer unto God thanksgiving; and pay thy vows unto the most High: And call upon me in the day of trouble: I will deliver thee, and thou shalt glorify me" (Ps. 50:14-15).

My response to the Word: I am completely thankful to the Lord, my God. In times of trouble, I will turn to Him, and I know He will deliver me. The results will bring glory to Him. Wonderful things happen to me when I pray with confidence. The Bible says, "And this is the confidence that we have in him, that, if we ask any thing according to his will, he heareth us: and if we know that he hear us, whatsoever we ask, we know that we have the petitions that we desired of him."

My prayer: Father, thank you for the multitude of prayer promises in your Word. I will turn to you as my first resort in times of trouble.

Today's Scriptures: Ps. 81:7; Ps. 107:6; Ps. 116:8; 1 John 5:14-15.

September 26

Today God says, *"I will show you My salvation."*

He promises me: "He shall call upon me, and I will answer him: I will be with him in trouble; I will deliver him, and honour him. With long life will I satisfy him, and shew him my salvation" (Ps. 91:15-16).

My response to the Word: God invites me to call upon Him, and He promises to answer my prayers. Furthermore, He promises to deliver me and to honor me. Then He goes a step further — He promises to give me long life, and to show me His salvation. Six promises in one Scripture verse! Each one is better than the other. The great love of my heavenly Father simply amazes me.

My prayer: Lord, I love you. Thank you for your promises of answered prayer, the help of your presence, your deliverance, honor, longevity, and salvation. I claim those promises as I pray. I praise you for your goodness to me.

Today's Scriptures: John 1:4; Phil. 2:16; Col. 3:4.

September 27

Today God says, *"I will be near you when you call upon Me in truth."*

He promises me: "The Lord is nigh unto all them that call upon him, to all that call upon him in truth" (Ps. 145:18).

My response to the Word: God promises to be near to me when I draw near to him. The Apostle James wrote, "Draw nigh to God, and he will draw nigh to you" (James 4:8). I will begin each day by drawing near to God, and I will continue to draw near to Him throughout each day. This is a wonderful promise: to know that Almighty God will come close to me when I call upon Him.

My prayer: Almighty Father, thank you for wanting to be near to me. Thank you for inviting me to draw near to you so that you can be near to me. I respond to that invitation in faith and truth.

Today's Scriptures: Ps. 4:1; Ps. 105:1; James 4:8; 1 Pet. 1:17.

September 28

Today God says, *"I will show you great and mighty things."*

He promises me: "Call unto me, and I will answer thee, and shew thee great and mighty things, which thou knowest not" (Jer. 33:3).

My response to the Word: God invites me to call upon Him. He promises to answer my prayers. Through prayer, I will learn many great and mighty spiritual things. I will remain open to all that God has for me throughout this day. I want to know more about His will, His ways, His purposes. God has so much in store for me.

My prayer: Father, thank you for wanting to reveal your truth to me. Help me to stay open for all you want to show me.

Today's Scriptures: John 16:13; Eph. 1:19; 1 Pet. 5:6.

September 29

Today God says, *"I am the horn of your salvation."*

He promises me: "The God of my rock; in him will I trust: he is my shield, and the horn of my salvation, my high tower, and my refuge, my saviour; thou savest me from violence. I will call on the Lord, who is worthy to be praised: so shall I be saved from mine enemies" (2 Sam. 22:3-4).

My response to the Word: God is the horn of my salvation. In fact, He is a cornucopia of blessings in my life. I love the Lord, and I know He loves me. The Bible says, "But God commendeth his love toward us, in that, while we were yet sinners, Christ died for us." Now I know I have salvation unto eternal life.

My prayer: Father, thank you for being the horn of my salvation. Through you I have found abundant and eternal life.

Today's Scriptures: Ps. 18:2; Luke 1:69; Rom. 5:8.

September 30

Today God says, *"You will find Me if you seek Me with all your heart."*

He promises me: "Then shall ye call upon me, and ye shall go and pray unto me, and I will hearken unto you. And ye shall seek me, and find me, when ye shall search for me with all your heart. And I will be found of you, saith the Lord: and I will turn away your captivity, and I will gather you from all the nations" (Jer. 29:12-14).

My response to the Word: God wants me to call upon Him and to pray. He promises me that He will listen to my voice as I do so. Furthermore, He invites me to seek Him, and He promises me that I will find Him when I do so. The prerequisite to these blessings is to search for Him with all my heart. I will search for the Lord with all my heart throughout this day.

My prayer: Heavenly Father, thank you for inviting me to seek you and search for you. Help me to do so with all my heart this day.

Today's Scriptures: Deut. 4:29; Prov. 8:17; Heb. 4:16.

October 1

Today God says, *"I will deliver you if you will call upon My name."*

He promises me: "And it shall come to pass, that whosoever shall call on the name of the Lord shall be delivered" (Joel 2:32).

My response to the Word: God promises to deliver everyone who calls upon His name. The word "deliverance" connotes taking someone from one place to a new place. It also suggests a transformation, a rescue, and a transaction that results in freedom. The Lord has delivered me from sin, Satan, fear, evil, and all things that hold me back from spiritual progress. He is a mighty Deliverer!

My prayer: O God, my Deliverer, thank you for setting me free. I will walk in the Promised Land of your victory throughout this day.

Today's Scriptures: Ps. 143:9; Isa. 61:1; Gal. 1:4.

October 2

Today God says, *"I know what you need before you ask Me."*

He promises me: "Your Father knoweth what things ye have need of, before ye ask him" (Matt. 6:8).

My response to the Word: God knows everything about me. He knows the number of hairs on my head. He knows my thoughts. He knows my heart. Even so, He wants me to pray, to seek His face, to petition Him for the things I need. Throughout this day I will remember that God never tires of hearing me pray.

My prayer: Thank you, Lord, for the power of prayer. I will spend more time in prayer today.

Today's Scriptures: John 16:30; Phil. 4:19; Heb. 4:16.

October 3

Today God says, *"Ask, and I will give it to you."*

He promises me: "Ask, and it shall be given you; seek, and ye shall find; knock, and it shall be opened unto you: For every one that asketh receiveth; and he that seeketh findeth; and to him that knocketh it shall be opened" (Matt. 7:7-8).

My response to the Word: The initials of ask, seek, and knock spell ASK — a helpful acronym that I will remember throughout this day as I ask, seek, and knock for those things I have need of. God promises me that when I ask for something (in accord with His will) He will give it to me. He says that if I will seek I will find, and when I knock the door will be opened. I realize that asking is a key to praying and receiving.

My prayer: Lord, thank you for the promises you have attached to asking, seeking, and knocking. Help me to remember to do these three things throughout this day.

Today's Scriptures: Mark 11:24; Luke 11:9; John 14:14; 1 John 3:22.

October 4
_____

Today God says, *"I will give good things to you when you ask me to do so."*

He promises me: "If ye then, being evil, know how to give good gifts unto your children, how much more shall your Father which is in heaven give good things to them that ask him?" (Matt 7:11).

My response to the Word: My loving Father promises to give me good things when I ask Him for them. I will remember the importance of prayer throughout this day, and I will believe that

God hears and answers my prayers because He wants to. I know that getting on my knees in prayer will help keep me on my toes spiritually.

My prayer: Father, thank you for being such a loving Father. I know you care about me and that you want to give me good things. Today I ask for the blessing of your presence.

Today's Scriptures: Mark 6:23; Luke 11:9; John 14:13.

October 5

Today God says, *"Whatever you pray for, believing, you shall receive."*

He promises me: "And all things, whatsoever ye shall ask in prayer, believing, ye shall receive" (Matt. 21:22).

My response to the Word: Believing prayer is true prayer. God says, "But without faith it is impossible to please him: for he that cometh to God must believe that he is, and that he is a rewarder of them that diligently seek him." Throughout this day I will pray in faith, because I know God answers prayers of faith.

My prayer: Lord, by faith I receive all that you have for me. I know you love me and want to bless me. Thank you for promising to answer my prayers of faith.

Today's Scriptures: Matt. 6:8; John 15:16; Heb. 11:6.

October 6

Today God says, *"I am your refuge."*

He promises me: "The God of my rock; in him will I trust: he is my shield, and the horn of my salvation, my high tower, and my refuge, my saviour; thou savest me from violence. I will call on the Lord, who is worthy to be praised: so shall I be saved from mine enemies" (2 Sam. 22:3-4).

My response to the Word: A refuge is a safe place which is free from threats of harm. God is my refuge from Satan, evil, the world, and sin. I will abide in Him. Jesus said, "Abide in me, and I in you. As the branch cannot bear fruit of itself, except it abide in the vine; no more can ye, except ye abide in me." I will abide in the Lord throughout this day.

My prayer: Lord, thank you for filling your Word with so many wonderful promises for me to claim. You are my refuge, and I will abide in you.

Today's Scriptures: Ps. 46:1; Ps. 91:2; Ps. 142:5; John 15:4.

October 7

Today God says, *"When you pray, believe that you have received what you have asked for, and I will give it to you."*

He promises me: "What things soever ye desire, when ye pray, believe that ye receive them, and ye shall have them" (Mark 11:24).

My response to the Word: Jesus gives this powerful prayer promise in the context of His teaching on the importance of faith. He said, "Have faith in God." Then He goes on to show that mountain-moving faith is possible for every believer. Throughout this passage He cautions us not to doubt, but to believe. Throughout this day I will believe God and His Word.

My prayer: Lord, thank you for the prayer promise that says you will grant my prayer requests when I pray in faith. With faith in my heart I now ask you for: _____
_____.

Today's Scriptures: Mark 9:23; Mark 11:22; James 1:6.

October 8

Today God says, *"I give you authority over the enemy."*

He promises me: "Behold, I give unto you power [authority] to tread on serpents and scorpions, and over all the power of the enemy: and nothing shall by any means hurt you" (Luke 10:19).

My response to the Word: Jesus has delegated authority to me for spiritual warfare. His authority enables me to conquer the enemy and keeps me from harm. He tells me to resist the devil and he will flee from me. My weapons are the name of Jesus, the blood of Jesus, and the Word of God.

My prayer: Lord, you are all-powerful. You are Almighty God. Thank you for imparting your power to me.

Today's Scriptures: Mark 16:17; Eph. 6:17; James 4:7; Rev. 12:11.

October 9

Today God says, *"If you will ask anything in the name of Jesus, I will do it."*

He promises me: "And whatsoever ye shall ask in my name, that will I do, that the Father may be glorified in the Son. If you shall ask any thing in my name, I will do it" (John 14:13-14).

My response to the Word: Jesus gives me the privilege of using His highly exalted name when I pray. The authority of His name represents everything Jesus is and has. He has given me the "power of attorney" to use His name when I petition the Father for my needs. Paul wrote,

"For there is one God, and one mediator between God and men, the man Christ Jesus: Who gave himself a ransom for all, to be testified in due time."

My prayer: Lord, thank you for the power of Jesus' name, and for permitting me to use His name when I pray. I will walk and pray in the power of Jesus' name throughout this day.

Today's Scriptures: John 15:16; Acts 3:6; 1 Tim. 2:5-6.

October 10

Today God says, *"Abide in Jesus, and let My Word abide in you, and I will answer your prayers."*

He promises me: "If ye abide in me, and my words abide in you, ye shall ask what ye will, and it shall be done unto you" (John 15:7).

My response to the Word: Jesus invites me to abide in Him. He is the Vine, and my heavenly Father is the vinedresser. God wants me to be a fruitful part of the vine, so He prunes me. His pruning in my life brings me closer to Jesus, the true Vine of life. It cleanses me and make me fruitful. Jesus said, "He that abideth in me, and I in him, the same bringeth forth much fruit: for without me ye can do nothing."

My prayer: Lord, thank you for grafting me into your vine of life. I will abide in Jesus throughout this day, realizing that this is a key to answered prayer.

Today's Scriptures: John 15:5; John 15:15; 1 John 2:6; 1 John 2:14.

October 11

Today God says, *"Pray in the name of Jesus, and your joy will be full."*

He promises me: "Hitherto have ye asked nothing in my name: ask, and ye shall receive, that your joy may be full" (John 16:24).

My response to the Word: Jesus invites me to pray in His name — a key to answered prayer. When I ask the Father for my needs to be met in the name of Jesus I will receive His answers, and my joy will be full. Nehemiah said, "The joy of the Lord is your strength." In Jesus' name I receive this promise of answered prayer and fullness of joy.

My prayer: Thank you, Lord, for promising to answer me when I pray in Jesus' name. This promise gives me joy, answered prayer gives me joy, and knowing you gives me joy.

Today's Scriptures: Neh. 8:10; John 14:13-14; Rom. 15:13; 1 Peter 1:8.

October 12

Today God says, *"My peace will keep your heart and mind through Christ Jesus."*

He promises me: "Be careful for nothing; but in every thing by prayer and supplication with thanksgiving let your requests be made known unto God. and the peace of God, which passeth all understanding, shall keep your hearts and minds through Christ Jesus" (Phil. 4:6-7).

My response to the Word: God's peace alleviates all anxiety and worry from my mind and heart. He commands me to stop worrying, to be thankful, and to pray. He promises that if I will take these steps, He will give me His peace — a peace that surpasses understanding. The peace of God will keep my heart and mind throughout this day.

My prayer: Lord, thank you for your promise of peace. I receive it by faith as I surrender all my concerns to you.

Today's Scriptures: Heb. 12:14; Heb. 13:20; 1 Pet. 5:14.

October 13

Today God says, *"I want you to rejoice evermore, to pray without ceasing, and to give thanks in everything."*

He promises me: "Rejoice evermore. Pray without ceasing. In every thing give thanks: for this is the will of God in Christ Jesus concerning you" (1 Thess. 5:16-18).

My response to the Word: I will rejoice, pray, and give thanks throughout this day, because I know this is the Father's will for me. Seldom does the Bible proclaim so precisely, "This is My will for you." God wants me to learn to live in praise and prayer because He knows this will give me greater happiness, success, and prosperity. I will obey His Word today.

My prayer: Lord, I rejoice in you because you invite me to pray and you promise to answer my prayers. Throughout this day I will remember to thank you and praise you.

Today's Scriptures: 2 Cor. 4:15; Phil. 4:6; Col. 2:7.

October 14

Today God says, *"I will be faithful in performing My Word to you."*

He promises me: "Faithful is he that calleth you, who also will do it" (1 Thess. 5:24).

My response to the Word: God is faithful. He has called me by His grace. He will perform in my life what His Word promises. Isaiah wrote, "So shall my word be that goeth forth out of my mouth: it shall not return unto me void, but it shall accomplish that which I please, and it shall prosper in the thing whereto I sent it."

My prayer: Lord, thank you for calling me out of the world or darkness, into the Kingdom of your marvelous light. I believe you will fulfill your Word in my life.

Today's Scriptures: Isa. 55:11; James 1:17; 1 Pet. 1:23.

October 15

Today God says, *"Pray for those in authority so that you can live a quiet and peaceful life."*

He promises me: "I exhort therefore, that, first of all, supplications, prayers, intercessions, and giving of thanks, be made for all men; For kings, and for all that are in authority; that we may lead a quiet and peaceable life in all godliness and honesty. For this is good and acceptable in the sight of God our Saviour" (1 Tim. 2:1-3).

My response to the Word: God wants me to lead a quiet and peaceable life in all godliness and honesty. He shows me that this will be possible if I will intercede faithfully in behalf of those in authority. He also wants me to be thankful for my leaders. I will remember to pray for those in positions of leadership at all levels of government, in the local church, in my workplace, and elsewhere. Truly, I am thankful for each one of them.

My prayer: Father, thank you for those you have placed in positions of authority. Bless them, guide them, and draw them closer to you. I intercede now for: _____

_____.

Today's Scriptures: Isa. 59:16; Rom. 8:26; Rom. 8:27.

October 16

Today God says, *"In your time of need, come before My throne, and I will give you mercy and grace."*

He promises me: "Let us therefore come boldly unto the throne of grace, that we may obtain mercy, and find grace to help in time of need" (Heb. 4:16).

My response to the Word: God sits upon His throne in heaven. His throne is a throne of grace. He invites me to come boldly (with great confidence) before His throne so that I will find His mercy and grace which will help me in my times of need. My confidence in prayer comes from this realization: "And this is the confidence that we have in him, that, if we ask any thing according to his will, he heareth us: And if we know that he hear us, whatsoever we ask, we know that we have the petitions that we desired of him."

My prayer: Lord, thank you for the confidence your Word imparts to me. When I pray to you I know you are hearing me, and I know you will grant my petitions.

Today's Scriptures: James 5:16; 1 John 4:15-16; 1 Pet. 4:7.

October 17

Today God says, *"Without faith it is impossible to please Me."*

He promises me: "But without faith it is impossible to please him: for he that cometh to God must believe that he is, and that he is a rewarder of them that diligently seek him" (Heb. 11:6).

My response to the Word: My God is a living God. My greatest desire is to please Him. I believe in Him and in His Word, and I also believe that He wants to reward my faith. Throughout this day, therefore, I will diligently seek Him. The Bible says, "Who through faith subdued kingdoms, wrought righteousness, obtained promises, stopped the mouths of lions, Quenched the violence of fire, escaped the edge of the sword, out of weakness were made strong, waxed valiant in fight, turned to flight the armies of the aliens . . . ." I will walk in the power of faith throughout this day.

My prayer: Lord, increase my faith as I seek you and study your Word. Thank you for rewarding my faith.

Today's Scriptures: Rom. 10:17; Heb. 6:12; Heb. 11:33-34; James 1:6-7; 1 Pet. 1:7.

October 18

Today God says, *"Ask Me for wisdom in faith, and I will give it to you."*

He promises me: "If any of you lack wisdom, let him ask of God, that giveth to all men liberally, and upbraideth not; and it shall be given him. But let him ask in faith, nothing wavering. For he that wavereth is like a wave of the sea driven with the wind and tossed" (James 1:5-6).

My response to the Word: God wants to impart His wisdom to me. He wants me to ask him for it. As I do so, I will remember to pray in faith, because I know God is a liberal Giver to those who ask Him in faith. With God's help, I will not waver in my faith, because I know, "A double minded man is unstable in all his ways."

My prayer: Lord, help me to be single-minded in my service to you, in prayer, and in everything

I say, think, and do. I ask for your wisdom to help me understand and deal with the following situation: _____

_____.

Today's Scriptures: James 1:8; James 3:17; 2 Pet. 3:9.

October 19

Today God says, *"You do not have certain things because you have not asked Me for them."*

He promises me: "Ye have not, because ye ask not" (James 4:2).

My response to the Word: The Apostle James simply states that asking is the key to receiving from God. He goes on to say, "Ye ask, and receive not, because ye ask amiss, that ye may consume it upon your lusts." It's important for me to remember how to ask, however. From my study of the Word, I know that I must ask in faith, with confidence, according to God's will, and I must abide in Jesus and let the Word of God abide in me. To do otherwise is to ask amiss.

My prayer: Father, teach me how to pray properly. I always want to please you.

Today's Scriptures: James 4:3; 1 John 3:23; 1 John 5:15-16.

October 20

Today God says, *"Submit yourself to Me, resist the devil, and he will flee from you."*

He promises me: "Submit yourselves therefore to God. Resist the devil, and he will flee from you" (James 4:7).

My response to the Word: Two main things give me spiritual victory: submitting myself to God and resisting the devil. I submit myself to God. I give Him my life, my body, my soul, my spirit, my work, my family, and everything else. Throughout this day I want to be fully surrendered to Him. In such a submitted relationship with God, I know the devil will flee when I resist him in faith.

My prayer: Father, I fully submit and surrender myself to you. You are my Lord. I give my life to you. Help me to resist the devil when he comes to tempt me.

Today's Scriptures: Luke 4:8; Luke 10:17; Heb. 12:9; 1 Pet. 2:13.

October 21

Today God says, *"The prayer of faith will save the sick, and I will raise them up."*

He promises me: And the prayer of faith shall save the sick, and the Lord shall raise him up" (James 5:15).

My response to the Word: The prayer of faith accomplishes a multitude of miracles. This is the mountain-moving kind of faith that Jesus speaks about. It gives me wisdom. It brings answers. It pleases God. It also brings God's healing power to the sick. God blesses the prayer of faith.

My prayer: Lord, I believe your Word. Your Word imparts faith to my heart. Therefore, I pray that you would minister your healing power to:

_____

_____.

Today's Scriptures: Matt. 21:22; Mark 11:23; Rom. 10:17; Heb. 11:6; James 1:6.

October 22

Today God says, *"Your effectual, fervent prayer will avail much."*

He promises me: "The effectual fervent prayer of a righteous man availeth much" (James 5:16).

My response to the Word: An effectual, fervent prayer is one that is adequate and effective (the prayer of faith), and it is sincere and filled with warm emotion (a knowledge of God's love). I am a righteous person, because God has imparted His righteousness to me. The Bible says, "But of him are ye in Christ Jesus, who of God is made unto us wisdom, and righteousness, and sanctification, and redemption."

My prayer: Lord, thank you for the righteousness that enables me to pray in faith in an effective and fervent manner. My prayers will avail much because you have promised this to me.

Today's Scriptures: 1 Cor. 1:30; Eph. 6:18; 1 Tim. 4:5.

October 23

Today God says, *"My eyes see you and My ears hear you."*

He promises me: "For the eyes of the Lord are over the righteous, and his ears are open unto their prayers" (1 Pet. 3:12).

My response to the Word: God sees everything about me — the things I do, the thoughts I think, the motives of my heart, and the feelings I experience. He cares about me, and He is intimately involved with all the details and concerns of my life. That's why He wants me to pray, and He promises to hear and answer my prayers.

My prayer: Dear Lord, thank you for watching over me, and for listening to my prayers. I want to have a closer relationship with you.

Today's Scriptures: Matt. 6:4; Matt. 6:6; Matt. 6:18.

October 24

Today God says, *"Keep My commandments, and I will answer your prayers."*

He promises me: "And whatsoever we ask, we receive of him, because we keep his commandments, and do those things that are pleasing in his sight" (1 John 3:22).

My response to the Word: God promises to answer my prayers when I walk in obedience to His Word. He wants me to do those things that please Him. His commandment is that I should believe the name of His Son Jesus Christ and love others. I commit myself to walking in obedience to His will throughout this day.

My prayer: Father, thank you for promising to answer my prayers when I walk in obedience to you and your Word. With your help, I will obey you at all times.

Today's Scriptures: Jer. 7:23; Jer. 42:6; Acts 5:32; 1 John 3:23-24.

October 25

Today God says, *"I always hear you when you pray according to My will."*

He promises me: "And this is the confidence that we have in him, that, if we ask any thing according to his will, he heareth us" (1 John 5:14).

My response to the Word: God hears me when I pray according to His will (His Word). Therefore, I will study to show myself approved unto God, a workman that does not ever need to be ashamed because I know how to rightly divide God's Word. God's Word is the bridge that spans the gap between God's way and my ways, God's thoughts and my thoughts.

My prayer: Lord, thank you for the confidence I have when I pray according to your will. I will pray your Word throughout this day.

Today's Scriptures: Ps. 34:15-17; Ps. 143:1; John 15:7; 2 Tim. 2:15.

October 26

Today God says, *"I am able to keep you from falling."*

He promises me: "Now unto him that is able to keep you from falling, and to present you faultless before the presence of his glory with exceeding joy, To the only wise God our Saviour, be glory and majesty, dominion and power, both now and ever. Amen" (Jude 24-25).

My response to the Word: God will keep me from falling, and He will present me faultless before the presence of His glory with exceeding joy. He is the only wise God, and He is my Savior. God will never allow anything to come to me that He and I cannot handle together. His Word declares: "There hath no temptation taken you but such as is common to man: but God is faithful, who will not suffer you to be tempted above that ye are able; but will with the temptation also make a way to escape, that ye may be able to bear it."

My prayer: Father, thank you for your promise to see me through every temptation and difficulty. I know you will be with me throughout this day.

Today's Scriptures: 1 Cor. 10:13; Eph. 3:20; James 1:12.

October 27

Today God says, *"You will overcome the devil by the blood of the Lamb and the word of your testimony."*

He promises me: "And they overcame him by the blood of the Lamb, and by the word of their testimony; and they loved not their lives unto the death" (Rev. 12:11).

My response to the Word: The blood of Jesus Christ cleanses me from all sin. The blood of Jesus enables me to draw near to God. I have been redeemed and delivered from the power of darkness through His blood. It also enables me to overcome the devil. Therefore, I will plead the merits of the blood of Jesus whenever temptation comes my way. I will testify that I am redeemed and have the victory through the precious blood of Christ. The Bible says, "Let the redeemed of the Lord say so, whom he hath redeemed from the hand of the enemy."

My prayer: Lord, thank you for redeeming me through the blood of the Lamb. I will avail myself of the power of His blood throughout this day.

Today's Scriptures: Ps. 107:2; Eph. 2:13; Col. 1:13-14; 1 John 1:7.

October 28

Today God says, *"I have washed you, regenerated you, and saved you through My mercy for you."*

He promises me: "Not by works of righteousness which we have done, but according to his mercy he saved us, by the washing of regeneration, and renewing of the Holy Ghost; Which he shed on us abundantly through Jesus Christ our Saviour" (Titus 3:5-6).

My response to the Word: God has been extremely merciful to me. He has saved me through the washing of regeneration and the renewing of the Holy Spirit through Jesus Christ, my Savior.

Throughout this day, therefore, I will obey the Word that tells me to: "Give thanks unto the Lord, for he is good: for his mercy endureth for ever."

My prayer: Thank you for your enduring mercy in my life, Father. I will walk in your mercy today, realizing that you have saved me, washed me, and renewed me through the power of your Holy Spirit.

Today's Scriptures: Ps. 107:1; Prov. 28:18; Rom. 10:13.

October 29

Today God says, *"I am rich in mercy and love for you."*

He promises me: "But God, who is rich in mercy, for his great love wherewith he loved us, Even when we were dead in sins, hath quickened us together with Christ, (by grace ye are saved;)" (Eph. 2:4-5).

My response to the Word: My Father is rich in mercy and love for me. What a tremendous thought that is! He loved me even when I was dead in sin, loved me so much, in fact, that He brought me to life in Christ. How thankful I am for His great salvation. "For by grace are ye saved through faith; and that not of yourselves: It is the gift of God: Not of works, lest any man should boast."

My prayer: Thank you, Lord, for saving my soul. Thank you, Lord, for making me whole. I give my life to you.

Today's Scriptures: Eph. 2:8-9; Titus 3:5; James 3:17.

October 30

Today God says, "*Your body is the temple of the Holy Spirit.*"

He promises me: "What? know ye not that your body is the temple of the Holy Ghost which is in you, which you have of God, and ye are not your own? For ye are bought with a price: therefore glorify God in your body, and in your spirit, which are God's" (1 Cor. 6:19-20).

My response to the Word: I am the temple of the Holy Spirit! I was redeemed by Jesus Christ who paid the price of His own life. I am no longer my own, but His. I have surrendered my right to self-interest, self-indulgence, self-aggrandizement, and all areas of selfishness that were a part of my life before He redeemed me. Throughout this day, therefore, I will glorify God in my body and spirit, fully realizing that they belong to God, not to me.

My prayer: Lord, thank you for redeeming me. Let the light of your Spirit radiate from my innermost being throughout this day.

Today's Scriptures: John 14:16-17; Rom. 12:1-2; 1 Cor. 7:23.

October 31

Today God says, *"Do not be confused; I will help you."*

He promises me: "For the Lord God will help me; therefore shall I not be confounded: therefore have I set my face like a flint, and I know that I shall not be ashamed" (Isa. 50:7).

My response to the Word: God promises to help me, even when I feel confused. At such times I will remember that He is never the author of confusion. He will help me. He gives me wisdom and a sound mind. I have set my face like a flint in the direction of all God has for me. He will never let me be confounded or ashamed.

My prayer: Lord, I trust you for wisdom and clear thinking every step of the way. I know you will help me in times of confusion so that I will not be confounded.

Today's Scriptures: Ps. 22:5; Prov. 2:7; 1 Cor. 14:33; 2 Tim. 1:7; 1 Pet. 2:6.

November 1

Today God says, *"I am love."*

He promises me: "Beloved, let us love one another: for love is of God; and every one that loveth is born of God, and knoweth God. He that loveth not knoweth not God; for God is love" (1 John 4:7-8).

My response to the Word: God is love, and He wants love to have the supreme place in my life. Love is the most excellent way. It is the highest law. Today I will walk in love, because I know the truth of Jesus' words: "By this shall all men know that ye are my disciples, if ye have love one to another."

My prayer: Heavenly Father, I know you are love, and you want me to walk in love. Let your love fill me so that it will overflow to everyone I see today.

Today's Scriptures: John 13:34-35; 1 Cor. 12:31; Eph. 5:1-2.

November 2

Today God says, *"Nothing will ever separate you from My love, which is in Christ Jesus."*

He promises me: "For I am persuaded, that neither death, nor life, nor angels, nor principalities, nor powers, nor things present, nor things to come, Nor height, nor depth, nor any other creature, shall be able to separate us from the love of God, which is in Christ Jesus our Lord" (Rom. 8:38-39).

My response to the Word: The love of God is deeper than the deepest ocean, and higher than the highest mountain. It is the greatest thing in the universe. He revealed His love to me through His Son, Jesus Christ, who expressed love wherever He went. I find God's love in Him, and I know that nothing shall ever be able to separate me from His love. That is a wonderful truth.

My prayer: Lord God, thank you for the assurance that I will never be separated from your love. I will walk in your love throughout this day.

Today's Scriptures: John 3:16; Gal. 2:20; Eph. 2:4.

November 3

Today God says, *"I will keep you in perfect peace if you will trust Me and keep your mind focused on Me."*

He promises me: "Thou wilt keep him in perfect peace, whose mind is stayed on thee: because he trusteth in thee" (Isa. 26:3).

My response to the Word: God is keeping me in perfect peace because I fully trust Him, and I keep my mind on Him. "For he is our peace, who hath made both one, and hath broken down the middle wall of partition between us." Jesus Christ is the Prince of peace, and I want to walk in His peace throughout this day.

My prayer: Heavenly Father, I choose the peace you offer instead of the restlessness of the world. Help me to stay focused on you throughout this day.

Today's Scriptures: Isa. 9:6; Eph. 2:14; 1 Pet. 5:14.

November 4

Today God says, *"I have removed your transgressions from you."*

He promises me: "As far as the east is from the west, so far hath he removed our transgressions from us" (Ps. 103:12).

My response to the Word: I no longer have to walk in shame or condemnation because God has already taken all my sins and transgressions from me. He has removed them as far from me as the east is from the west. His Word declares: "There is therefore now no condemnation to them which are in Christ Jesus, who walk not after the flesh, but after the Spirit."

My prayer: Lord, thank you for taking all condemnation, guilt, and fear from me. I will walk in true spiritual freedom throughout this day.

Today's Scriptures: Rom. 8:1-2; Eph. 4:32; Col. 2:13.

November 5

Today God says, *"Forgive others, and I will forgive you."*

He promises me: "And when ye stand praying, forgive, if ye have ought against any: that your Father also which is in heaven may forgive you your trespasses" (Mark 11:25).

My response to the Word: When Jesus taught His disciples to pray (the Lord's Prayer), He showed them the importance of forgiveness: "And forgive us our debts, as we forgive our debtors." For my Father in heaven to forgive me as I forgive others is a sobering thought. It stresses the importance of forgiving others. I will walk in God's love and forgiveness throughout this day.

My prayer: Lord, thank you for forgiving me of all my sins. Help me to forgive others in the same way you have forgiven me.

Today's Scriptures: Matt. 6:12; Eph. 1:7; Col. 1:14.

November 6

Today God says, *"If you confess your sins, I will forgive you."*

He promises me: "If we confess our sins, he is faithful and just to forgive us our sins, and to cleanse us from all unrighteousness" (1 John 1:9).

My response to the Word: God is so good to me. He promises to forgive me of my sins when I confess them to Him. He also promises to cleanse me from all unrighteousness. God's forgiveness in my life is the key that unlocks the door of resentment and the handcuffs of hate. It is a power that breaks the chains of bitterness and the shackles of selfishness. I am so thankful that God forgives me and cleanses me.

My prayer: Lord, I confess my sins to you: __
_____
_____
_____. Thank you for forgiving me and cleansing me from all unrighteousness.

Today's Scriptures: Ps. 32:5; Prov. 28:13; James 5:16.

November 7

Today God says, *"In Christ, you are My righteousness."*

He promises me: "For he hath made him to be sin for us, who knew no sin; that we might be made the righteousness of God in him" (2 Cor. 5:21).

My response to the Word: The spotless Lamb of God became sin on the cross for me. He carried all my sin and guilt and shame with Him so that I could become the righteousness of God in Him. This is an amazing truth. Jesus became sin so I could become righteousness. The Bible says, "But of him are ye in Christ Jesus, who of God is made unto us wisdom, and righteousness, and sanctification, and redemption."

My prayer: Loving God, thank you for sending Jesus to take all my sins away and to make me righteous. He is my wisdom, righteousness, sanctification, and redemption. Glory to His name.

Today's Scriptures: 1 Cor. 1:30; 2 Cor. 5:21; Phil. 1:11.

November 8

Today God says, *"My truth will make you free."*

He promises me: "And ye shall know the truth, and the truth shall make you free. If the Son therefore shall make you free, ye shall be free indeed" (John 8:32, 36).

My response to the Word: The truth of God's Word sets me free from all deception, sin, and evil. There is no substitute for God's truth, and realizing this, I will walk in God's truth throughout this day. Jesus is the way, the truth, and the life. He has given His Spirit of truth to me. I will let His truth be my guide in all that I say, think, and do today.

My prayer: Lord, I thank you for your truth which has set me free. Let its light guide me all day long.

Today's Scriptures: John 14:6-7; John 14:17; Eph. 1:13; Eph. 4;15.

November 9

Today God says, *"I will fight for you."*

He promises me: "The Lord your God which goeth before you, he shall fight for you, according to all that he did for you in Egypt before your eyes" (Deut. 1:30).

My response to the Word: God goes before me, He fights for me, and He helps me to fight the battles that confront me. He is a miracle-working Father who possesses all power in heaven and earth. God is my Guardian. He promises, "When thou passest through the waters, I will be with thee; and through the rivers, they shall not overflow thee: when thou walkest through the fire, thou shalt not be burned; neither shall the flame kindle upon thee."

My prayer: Lord, thank you for being willing to fight for me. I realize that you will always help me to be victorious.

Today's Scriptures: Exod. 14:25; Josh. 23:10; Isa. 43:2.

November 10

Today God says, "*I am your shelter and your strong tower.*"

He promises me: "For thou hast been a shelter for me, and a strong tower from the enemy" (Ps. 61:3).

My response to the Word: God is my shelter from all stormy blasts that the enemy would try to unleash in my life. The Bible says, "The eternal God is thy refuge, underneath are the everlasting arms: and he shall thrust out the enemy from before thee; and shall say, Destroy them."

My prayer: Father, thank you for being my shelter. Throughout this day I will remain in the shelter of your wings.

Today's Scriptures: Deut. 33:27; Ps. 18:2; Ps. 91:1; Prov. 18:10.

November 11

Today God says, "*When the enemy comes in like a flood, My Spirit will raise a standard against him.*"

He promises me: "So shall they fear the name of the Lord from the west, and his glory from the rising of the sun. When the enemy shall come in like a flood, the Spirit of the Lord shall lift up a standard against him" (Isa. 59:19).

My response to the Word: The adversary of my life is Satan. Jesus said, "The thief cometh not, but for to steal, and to kill, and to destroy; I am come that they might have life, and that they might have it more abundantly." Satan is already a defeated foe. He has no right to any aspect of my life because I am a redeemed child of God.

My prayer: Lord, thank you for your promise to overcome the enemy in every area of my life. I know you are lifting a standard against him in my behalf.

Today's Scriptures: Luke 10:19; John 10:10; Col. 1:13; Rev. 12:11.

November 12

Today God says, *"I will keep you by My power."*

He promises me: "Who are kept by the power of God through faith unto salvation ready to be revealed in the last time" (1 Pet. 1:5).

My response to the Word: God's power is able to keep me through faith. This knowledge gives me a sense of deep and lasting security. Paul wrote, "But the Lord is faithful, who shall stablish you, and keep you from evil." Because I know God is keeping me, I will keep on keeping on.

My prayer: Father, thank you for your keeping power in my life. I place my life securely in your hands.

Today's Scriptures: Ps. 121:5; Prov. 13:6; 2 Thess. 3:3.

November 13

Today God says, *"The hope I give to you is an anchor for your soul."*

He promises me: ". . . who have fled for refuge to lay hold upon the hope set before us: Which hope we have as an anchor of the soul, both sure and stedfast, and which entereth into that within the veil" (Heb. 6:18-19).

My response to the Word: God gives me hope. It is the anchor of my soul during the storms of life. Hope sees the invisible, feels the intangible, and achieves the impossible. Hope is faith holding out its hand in the dark. Hope is the anchor of the soul, the stimulus to action, and the incentive to achievement. I will walk in hope throughout this day.

My prayer: Lord, thank you for giving me hope that eagerly expects good things from you. The hope you impart to me keeps me stedfast in times of stress.

Today's Scriptures: Prov. 10:28; Lam. 3:24; Rom. 5:5; Rom. 15:13.

November 14

Today God says, *"I will give you sufficiency in all things."*

He promises me: "And God is able to make all grace abound toward you; that ye, always having all sufficiency in all things, may abound to every good work" (2 Cor. 9:8).

My response to the Word: God's grace is sufficient for me. Sufficiency involves the complete satisfaction of a need, and through God's grace I am able to experience sufficiency in all things so that I will abound to every good work. It is God's grace that keeps me, sanctifies me, saves me, and meets my need. I will walk in God's all-sufficient grace throughout this day.

My prayer: Lord, thank you for your grace which is at work in my life continually. Through your grace I will learn how to abound in every good work.

Today's Scriptures: John 15:16; 2 Cor. 3:5; 2 Cor. 12:9.

November 15

Today God says, *"My strength is made perfect in weakness."*

He promises me: "And he said unto me, My grace is sufficient for thee: for my strength is made perfect in weakness. Most gladly therefore will I rather glory in my infirmities, that the power of Christ may rest upon me" (2 Cor. 12:9).

My response to the Word: The Father's grace and strength are constantly at work in my life. He perfects His strength in my times of weakness. This knowledge is what enables Paul to say, "When I am weak, then am I strong." It is also the reason Paul was able to say, "I can do all things through Christ which strengtheneth me." I will walk in God's strength throughout this day.

My prayer: Lord, thank you for your strength which is made perfect in my weakness. Empower me to do your will throughout this day.

Today's Scriptures: 2 Cor. 12:10; Phil. 4:13; 1 Pet. 5:10.

November 16

Today God says, *"Through My promises you are able to partake of the divine nature."*

He promises me: "Whereby are given unto us exceeding great and precious promises: that by these ye might be partakers of the divine nature, having escaped the corruption that is in the world through lust" (2 Pet. 1:4).

My response to the Word: God's exceedingly great and precious promises are for me to claim, appropriate, and live by. He blesses me with these promises so that I would become a partaker of His divine nature and I would be able to escape the corruption of the world. God's promises are like promissory notes; they mature over a period of time. I will walk upon the promises of God throughout this day.

My prayer: Lord, thank you for your great and precious promises which enable me to partake of your nature. I believe your Word, and I claim its promises for my life this day.

Today's Scriptures: 2 Cor. 1:20; 2 Cor. 7:1; Heb. 6:12.

November 17

Today God says, *"I forgive all your iniquities, and I heal all your diseases."*

He promises me: "Bless the Lord, O my soul, and forget not all his benefits: Who forgiveth all thine iniquities; who healeth all thy diseases; Who redeemeth thy life from destruction; who crowneth thee with lovingkindness and tender mercies" (Ps. 103:2-4).

My response to the Word: The multitude of God's blessings in my life exceeds my memory's ability to contain them all. He has been and continues to be so wonderful to me. Throughout this day, therefore, I will command my soul to bless Him because I know He has forgiven me all my iniquities and He heals all my diseases. He has redeemed my life from destruction, and He has crowned me with lovingkindness and His tender mercies.

My prayer: Dear Father, thank you for all the benefits you've given to me. I will walk in awareness of your lovingkindness and tender mercies throughout this day.

Today's Scriptures: Luke 5:21; James 5:15; 1 John 1:9.

November 18

Today God says, "*I will renew your youth like the eagle's.*"

He promises me: "Who satisfieth thy mouth with good things; so that thy youth is renewed like the eagle's" (Ps. 103:5).

My response to the Word: God supplies all my needs. He satisfies me with so many good things, and He promises to rejuvenate me with His power. Paul wrote, "But if the Spirit of him that raised up Jesus from the dead dwell in you, he that raised up Christ form the dead shall also quicken your mortal bodies by his Spirit that dwelleth in you."

My prayer: Thank you, Lord, for satisfying my mouth with good things, and for renewing my youth like the eagle's. I will praise you for your blessings throughout this day.

Today's Scriptures: Rom. 8:11; 2 Cor. 4:16; Eph. 4:23.

November 19

Today God says, *"I will guide you continually."*

He promises me: "And the Lord shall guide thee continually, and satisfy thy soul in drought, and make fat thy bones: and thou shalt be like a watered garden, and like a spring of water, whose waters fail not" (Isa. 58:11).

My response to the Word: God is guiding me continually and He is satisfying my soul. He promises to make my life like a watered garden and like an unfailing spring. I claim these promises for my life today. I trust God to guide me each step of the way. Paul wrote, "For as many as are led by the Spirit of God, they are the sons of God."

My prayer: Father, thank you for guiding me continually. Guide me throughout this day.

Today's Scriptures: Ps. 25:9; Ps. 32:8; Rom 8:14.

November 20

Today God says, *"I will freely give you all things."*

He promises me: "He that spared not his own Son, but delivered him up for us all, how shall he not with him also freely give us all things?" (Rom. 8:32).

My response to the Word: God did not spare His own Son, but gave Him up for me. The Word says, "For God so loved the world, that he gave his only begotten Son, that whosoever believeth in him should not perish, but have everlasting life." The fact that God loved the world so much that He gave up His only begotten Son for me shows me that God's essence is love, and He loves so much that He always gives.

My prayer: Father, thank you for your giving love in my life. I receive all that you have for me so that I can share it with others.

Today's Scriptures: John 3:16; 1 Cor. 1:4; Gal. 2:9.

November 21

Today God says, *"I have already blessed you with all spiritual blessings."*

He promises me: "Blessed be the God and Father of our Lord Jesus Christ, who hath blessed us with all spiritual blessings in heavenly places in Christ" (Eph. 1:3).

My response to the Word: Every spiritual blessing that exists has already been imparted to me. All I need to do is to believe this promise, receive it, and let it become actualized in my life through prayer and cooperation with God. This I will do throughout this day as I reflect on all the spiritual blessings God has already imparted to me.

My prayer: Lord, I love you and I praise you. Thank you for every spiritual blessing you have given to me. Help me to walk in them each step of the way.

Today's Scriptures: Prov. 10:22; Mal. 3:10; 1 Pet. 3:9.

November 22

Today God says, *"Old things have passed away; behold, all things are new in your life."*

He promises me: "Therefore if any man be in Christ, he is a new creature: old things are passed away; behold, all things are become new" (2 Cor. 5:17).

My response to the Word: God is transforming me through His Word and His Spirit. I truly am a new creation in Christ Jesus. I will let the old things pass away, and I will walk in newness of life throughout this day. I will remember the truth of God's Word: "And God is able to make all grace abound toward you; that ye, always having all sufficiency in all things, may abound to every good work."

My prayer: Lord, thank you for transforming my life so completely. With your help, Father, I will walk in newness of life throughout this day.

Today's Scriptures: 2 Cor. 9:8; Eph. 4:23-24; Col. 3:10.

November 23

Today God says, *"I daily load you with benefits."*

He promises me: "Blessed be the Lord, who daily loadeth us with benefits, even the God of our salvation" (Ps. 68:19).

My response to the Word: My heart swells with thanksgiving when I realize the truth that God literally loads me with benefits each day. Throughout this day I will strive to be like the Psalmist who said, "Bless the Lord, O my soul: and all that is within me, bless his holy name. Bless the Lord, O my soul, and forget not all his benefits."

My prayer: Lord, I do bless you for all the good things you've given to me. You have forgiven all my iniquities, healed my diseases, and redeemed my life from destruction. Praise your holy name!

Today's Scriptures: Ps. 103:1-2; Ps. 116:12; 1 Tim. 6:6.

November 24

Today God says, *"All Scripture is given by My inspiration."*

He promises me: "All Scripture is given by inspiration of God, and is profitable for doctrine, for reproof, for correction, for instruction in righteousness" (2 Tim. 3:16).

My response to the Word: God has inspired His Word so that it can be a profitable spiritual tool in my life. It brings me teaching and correction. "For the word of God is quick, and powerful, and sharper than any two-edged sword, piercing even to the dividing asunder of soul and spirit, and of the joints and marrow, and is a discerner of the thoughts and intents of the heart." Throughout this day I will let the Word of God do its work in my life.

My prayer: Heavenly Father, thank you for the treasure chest of your Word. It is my infallible rule for faith and practice.

Today's Scriptures: Col. 1:5; Col. 3:16; Titus 1:9; Heb. 4:12.

November 25

Today God says, *"My Word will never return unto Me void."*

He promises me: "So shall my word be that goeth forth out of my mouth: it shall not return unto me void, but it shall accomplish that which I please, and its shall prosper in the thing whereto I sent it" (Isa. 55:11).

My response to the Word: God's Word is so powerful that it has to accomplish its purposes in my life. I will let it have full sway in my heart and soul so that I can receive all its blessings. I believe, "Every word of God is pure: he is a shield unto them that put their trust in him." I also know this truth: "For ever, O Lord, thy word is settled in heaven."

My prayer: Lord, let your Word do its dynamic work in my life. I believe your Word, and I know it will accomplish your eternal purposes.

Today's Scriptures: Ps. 119:89; Prov. 30:5; 1 Pet. 1:23.

November 26

Today God says, *"I have prepared so many wonderful things for you."*

He promises me: "But as it is written, Eye hath not seen, nor ear heard, neither have entered into the heart of man, the things which God hath prepared for them that love him" (1 Cor. 2:9).

My response to the Word: God has already prepared so many wonderful things for me. Jesus said, "I go to prepare a place for you. And if I go and prepare a place for you, I will come again, and receive you unto myself; that where I am, there ye may be also." The Bible also says, "God is not ashamed to be called their God: for he hath prepared for them a city."

My prayer: Father God, thank you for preparing so many things for me, both in this life and in the life to come. It is truly wonderful to be your child in your Kingdom.

Today's Scriptures: John 14:2-3; Heb. 11:6; Heb. 11:16.

November 27

Today God says, *"I will guide you with My eye."*

He promises me: "I will instruct thee and teach thee in the way which thou shalt go: I will guide thee with mine eye" (Ps. 32:8).

My response to the Word: God's guidance in my life keeps me on the right track. "He leadeth me in the paths of righteousness for his name's sake." I believe His Word which declares: "The steps of a good man are ordered by the Lord: and he delighteth in his way." I will let God guide me each step of the way.

My prayer: Heavenly Father, lead me and guide me as I go about my daily activities. It is such an adventure to be led by you.

Today's Scriptures: Ps. 23:3; Ps. 37:23; John 16:13.

November 28

Today God says, *"My promises never fail."*

He promises me: "Blessed be the Lord, that hath given rest unto his people Israel, according to all that he promised: there hath not failed one word of all his good promise" (1 Kings 8:56).

My response to the Word: I totally depend on God's promises. I stand upon them, walk upon them, believe them, trust them, and live them. They form the most solid foundation possible. They assure me of this continuing truth: "If God be for us, who can be against us?" I will walk according to God's promises throughout this day.

My prayer: Lord, thank you for your promises which are a sure foundation on which I build my life. As I meditate upon your promises I realize how truly blessed I am.

Today's Scriptures: Rom. 8:31; 2 Cor. 1:20; 2 Pet. 1:4.

November 29

Today God says, *"My everlasting arms are beneath you."*

He promises me: "The eternal God is thy refuge, and underneath are the everlasting arms: and he shall thrust out the enemy from before thee; and shall say, Destroy them" (Deut. 33:27).

My response to the Word: God is my eternal refuge. His everlasting arms hold me up. He promises to cast the enemy out of my way. With this understanding of who God is I am able to go forth in great peace and confidence, because He will hold me up and fight for me. I know that He will help me to do whatever He wants me to do.

My prayer: Father God, I need your help every moment of every day. Thank you for being so directly involved in every aspect of my life.

Today's Scriptures: Ps. 89:13; Ps. 125:1; Isa. 51:9.

November 30

Today God says, *"I will renew your strength."*

He promises me: "But they that wait upon the Lord shall renew their strength; they shall mount up with wings as eagles; they shall run, and not be weary; and they shall walk, and not faint" (Isa. 40:31).

My response to the Word: Throughout this day I will wait upon the Lord, because I know this is the key to receiving His strength in my life. "I can do all things through Christ which strengtheneth me." God is the strength of my life. "He giveth power to the faint; and to them that have no might he increaseth strength." I will walk in God's strength today.

My prayer: Father, strengthen me according to your Word. Thank you for the strength you give to me as I wait upon you.

Today's Scriptures: Isa. 40:29; Luke 1:51; 2 Cor. 12:9; Phil 4:13.

December 1

Today God says, *"I want you to enter into My rest."*

He promises me: "There remaineth therefore a rest to the people of God" (Heb. 4:9).

My response to the Word: God wants me to enter into His rest, but there are three things that will keep me out of it: disobedience, hardness of heart, and unbelief. Therefore, I will be careful to walk in obedience, faith, and openness before the Lord throughout this day. The Word of God declares: "Great peace have they which love thy law: and nothing shall offend them."

My prayer: Lord God, thank you for the rest you have given to me. I will trust you, believe your promises, and remain open to all you have for me throughout this day.

Today's Scriptures: Ps. 119:165; Heb. 4:9; Heb. 4:10.

December 2

Today God says, *"I am with you."*

He promises me: "Fear thou not; for I am with thee: be not dismayed; for I am thy God: I will strengthen thee; yea, I will help thee: yea, I will uphold thee with the right hand of my right-eousness" (Isa. 41:10).

My response to the Word: The knowledge that God is ever-present with me takes away all fear and anxiety from my life. His promise to strengthen me and help me fills me with confidence. Therefore, I will not fear either today or tomorrow because I know God is already there. In fact, He is the God who is always with me.

My prayer: Lord, thank you for being my ever-present strength. Thank you for upholding me with your righteousness.

Today's Scriptures: Ps. 46:1; Ps. 139:7; 1 Thess. 2:19.

December 3

Today God says, *"If you will humble yourself under My hand, I will lift you up."*

He promises me: "Humble yourselves there-fore under the mighty hand of God, that he may exalt you in due time: Casting all your care upon him; for he careth for you" (1 Pet. 5:6-7).

My response to the Word: Throughout this day I will humble myself under God's mighty hand, because I know this is a key to blessing in my life. I will cast all my worries and anxieties upon Him, because I know He does care about me. I know that if I will bow humbly before God, my Creator, He will lift me up into His perfect plan for my life.

My prayer: Dear Father God, give me the grace of humility as I go about my daily activities. I submit myself to your Lordship.

Today's Scriptures: Matt. 18:4; James 4:6; 1 Pet. 5:6.

December 4

Today God says, *"I will deliver you from temptation."*

He promises me: "The Lord knoweth how to deliver the godly out of temptations" (2 Pet. 2:9).

My response to the Word: God promises to strengthen me in the face of every temptation. He proclaims, "For sin shall not have dominion over you: for ye are not under the law, but under grace." The temptations I face are common to people everywhere, but God is faithful to me, and He promises not to let me be tempted beyond my ability to endure.

My prayer: God, thank you for helping me to overcome temptations in my life. You are so very faithful to me.

Today's Scriptures: Rom. 6:14; 1 Cor. 10:13; Heb. 2:18.

December 5

Today God says, *"The trying of your faith will work patience into you."*

He promises me: "My brethren, count it all joy when ye fall into divers temptations; Knowing this, that the trying of your faith worketh patience" (James 1:2-3).

My response to the Word: The trying of my faith is much more precious than gold. When times of temptation and tribulation come it's difficult to be joyful, but when I realize that these experiences build patient endurance into me, I regain my joy. The joy of the Lord is not a fickle emotion that is based on the circumstance I'm experiencing; rather, it is an abiding happiness that comes from the knowledge that God has everything under control.

My prayer: Lord, thank you for working patience into my life through the trials I face. I will walk in your joy today.

Today's Scriptures: Neh. 8:10; 1 Pet. 1:7; 1 Pet. 4:12-13.

December 6

Today God says, *"I have adopted you into My family."*

He promises me: "For ye have not received the spirit of bondage again to fear; but ye have received the Spirit of adoption, whereby we cry, Abba, Father" (Rom. 8:15).

My response to the Word: God has adopted me into His family, and now I am His child. The Bible says, "But as many as received him, to them gave he power to become the sons of God, even to them that believe on his name." I believe on the name of Jesus Christ, and I have received Him into my life. God has empowered me to be His child, and this fact makes me want to cry out, "Abba, Father."

My prayer: Lord, it is such a privilege for me to be your child. Thank you for your loving Fatherhood in my life.

Today's Scriptures: John 1:12; Gal. 4:5; Eph. 1:5.

December 7

Today God says, *"There is no fear in love."*

He promises me: "There is no fear in love; but perfect love casteth out fear: because fear hath torment. He that feareth is not made perfect in love" (1 John 4:18).

My response to the Word: One of the greatest mistakes I can ever make is to be constantly fearful that I will make a mistake. God's love removes that fear from me. Though I do not know what the future holds, I do know who holds the future. This knowledge gives me a feeling of hope, security, and confidence, because I know God loves me.

My prayer: Heavenly Father, you are love. Fill me with your love throughout this day.

Today's Scriptures: 2 Cor. 13:14; 1 Tim. 1:14; 1 John 4:10.

December 8

Today God says, *"Everlasting joy shall be upon your head."*

He promises me: "Therefore the redeemed of the Lord shall return, and come with singing unto Zion; and everlasting joy shall be upon their head: they shall obtain gladness and joy; and sorrow and mourning shall flee away" (Isa. 51:11).

My response to the Word: Everlasting joy! What a promise that is! Joy that never ceases —

this is God's promise to me. I will walk in His joy throughout this day, and as I do so, all sorrow and mourning shall flee away. I will keep my heart free from hate, my mind free from worry, and my mouth free from corrupt words. I will rejoice in the Lord. In this way, everlasting joy will be upon my head.

My prayer: God, help me to walk in your everlasting joy throughout this day. Thank you for your promise of joy and gladness.

Today's Scriptures: Rom. 14:17; Gal. 5:22; Phil. 4:4; 1 John 1:4.

December 9

Today God says, *"Jesus Christ shall return."*

He promises me: "For ye have need of patience, that, after ye have done the will of God, ye might receive the promise. For yet a little while, and he that shall come will come, and will not tarry" (Heb. 10:36-37).

My response to the Word: The Second Coming of Christ is an imminent reality. The Lord will return, and the dead in Christ will rise up to meet Him first; then we which remain will be caught up in the clouds together with them, and so shall we ever be with the Lord. This is both an exciting and comforting truth.

My prayer: Father God, thank you for sending Jesus to live and die for me, and thank you for the promise that He will come again. I look forward to His coming.

Today's Scriptures: John 14:1-6; 1 Thess. 4:15-18; Rev. 22:20.

December 10

Today God says, *"I know the secrets of your heart."*

He promises me: "If we have forgotten the name of our God, or stretched out our hands to a strange god; Shall not God search this out? for he knoweth the secrets of the heart" (Ps. 44:20-21).

My response to the Word: It isn't a frightening or intimidating thought to realize that God knows the secrets of my heart. In many ways, it is actually comforting, because if He knows all about me, He knows exactly what I need. I know that my loving heavenly Father has a wonderful plan for my life, and throughout this day I will cooperate with Him.

My prayer: "Search me, O God, and know my heart: try me, and know my thoughts: And see if there be any wicked way in me, and lead me in the way everlasting."

Today's Scriptures: Ps. 139:23-24; Rom. 2:16; 1 Cor. 14:25.

December 11

Today God says, *"I am the Father of lights; I do not change."*

He promises me: "Every good gift, and every perfect gift is from above, and cometh down from the Father of lights, with whom is no variableness, neither shadow of turning" (James 1:17).

My response to the Word: God never changes. He is the same yesterday, today, and tomorrow. His immutability (unchanging nature) gives me something to hold onto during times of transition and stress. God is the Giver of every good and perfect gift, and He has given so many gifts to me. I will walk in the knowledge of His unchanging stability throughout this day.

My prayer: Lord, thank you for always being there and for always being the same. I am so glad that you never change.

Today's Scriptures: Ps. 46:1; Mal. 3:6; Heb. 13:8.

December 12

Today God says, *"My Word gives you life."*

He promises me: "This is my comfort in my affliction: for thy word hath quickened me" (Ps. 119:50).

My response to the Word: God's Word is alive, and it gives me spiritual life as well. I will walk in the life of God's Word throughout this day as I contemplate its amazing power in my life: "For the word of God is quick, and powerful, and sharper than any two-edged sword, piercing even to the dividing asunder of soul and spirit, and of the joints and marrow, and is a discerner of the thoughts and intents of the heart."

My prayer: God, thank you for your powerful, living Word. I will meditate upon its precepts throughout this day. Quicken me according to your Word.

Today's Scriptures: Ps. 119:25; Phil. 2:16; Heb. 4:12; 1 John 1:1.

December 13

Today God says, *"The day will come when you will have no more pain, tears, death, or sorrow."*

He promises me: "And God shall wipe away all tears from their eyes; and there shall be no more death, neither sorrow, nor crying, neither shall there be any more pain: for the former things are passed away" (Rev. 21:4).

My response to the Word: In the heavenly kingdom, where I will live with God and my fellow-believers throughout eternity, there will be no more crying, pain, sorrow, or death. What a place that will be! Throughout this day I will remember that God has two dwelling places — one in heaven, and the other in a meek and thankful heart.

My prayer: Father, thank you for the promise of living with you forever in the kingdom of heaven. I greatly look forward to that blessed time of everlasting joy and peace in your presence.

Today's Scriptures: Eph. 1:3; Eph. 2:6; 2 Tim. 4:18.

December 14

Today God says, *"What I have spoken I will bring to pass."*

He promises me: "My counsel shall stand, and I will do all my pleasure. . . . I have spoken it, I will also bring it to pass; I have purposed it, I will also do it" (Isa. 46:10-11).

My response to the Word: God has plans and purposes for my life. He will be sure that His plans and purposes are accomplished. He always fulfills His promises to me. Throughout this day, therefore, I will remember these words: "Faithful is he that calleth you, who also will do it."

My prayer: Lord, I am so grateful for your faithfulness in my life. I believe every promise in your Word, because I know you will bring to pass everything that you have spoken.

Today's Scriptures: Ps. 89:1; Ps. 119:90; Lam. 3:23; 1 Thess. 5:24.

December 15

Today God says, *"My way is perfect."*

He promises me: "As for God, his way is perfect: the word of the Lord is tried: he is a buckler to all those that trust in him" (Ps. 18:30).

My response to the Word: God's way is perfect, and so is His timing. His Word is infallible. Because of these facts of my faith, I know that He will be my buckler — a shield that deflects all fiery darts of evil. Paul wrote, "Above all, taking the shield of faith, wherewith ye shall be able to quench all the fiery darts of the wicked."

My prayer: Lord, I know you are perfect, your Word is perfect, your will is perfect, and your way is perfect. I submit my life to you.

Today's Scriptures: 2 Sam. 22:31; Ps. 19:7; Eph. 6:16.

December 16

Today God says, *"I will make your feet like hinds' feet."*

He promises me: "The Lord God is my strength, and he will make my feet like hinds' feet, and he will make me to walk upon mine high places" (Hab. 3:19).

My response to the Word: The hind (a young deer) is a sure-footed animal that is able to walk along narrow rock ledges and other difficult spots without fear. God promises to make my feet like those of the hind, and He gives me the confidence to do so. Therefore, I will not cast away my confidence throughout this day.

My prayer: Lord, thank you for being my strength. Help me to be sure-footed wherever I go today.

Today's Scriptures: 1 Thess. 3:13; 2 Thess. 2:17; 2 Thess. 3:3; Heb. 10:35.

December 17

Today God says, *"I am your stronghold in the day of trouble."*

He promises me: "The Lord is good, a strong hold in the day of trouble; and he knoweth them that trust in him" (Nah. 1:7).

My response to the Word: God is so good to me, and I trust Him with everything I am and have. He is the stronghold I need in times of trouble. He keeps me safe. With God's help, I will be sure to let life's difficulties make me into a better person, not into a bitter person. Even if other people are preoccupied with adding up their troubles, I will purpose to count my blessings.

My prayer: I know, Lord, that you will always be with me during times of trouble and difficulty; therefore, I will not fear such times. Thank you for being my stronghold.

Today's Scriptures: Ps. 71:3; Ps. 89:8; Ps. 136:12.

December 18

Today God says, *"Jesus Christ is the same yesterday, today, and forever."*

He promises me: "Jesus Christ the same yesterday, and today, and for ever" (Heb. 13:8).

My response to the Word: The fact that Jesus Christ never changes works stability into my own life. This means He has the power to heal, to restore, to redeem, to save, to deliver, and to give victory just as He had when He walked the earth. Luke wrote, "And the whole multitude sought to touch him: for there went virtue out of him, and healed them all." Jesus is the Great Physician, and He is my Healer.

My prayer: Loving Lord, thank you for the constancy of Jesus Christ. I receive His power into my life.

Today's Scriptures: Mal. 3:6; Luke 6:19; James 1:17.

December 19

Today God says, *"Meditate upon My Word, and I will bless you with prosperity."*

He promises me: "This book of the law shall not depart out of thy mouth; but thou shalt meditate therein day and night, that thou mayest observe to do according to all that is written therein: for then thou shalt make thy way prosperous, and then thou shalt have good success" (Josh. 1:8).

My response to the Word: God's Word is life to me. I will meditate upon it, speak it, and live it throughout this day. God promises me that if I will do these things, He will make my way prosperous and give me success. This coincides with what the Psalmist wrote: "But his delight is in the law of the Lord; and in his law doth he meditate day and night. And he shall be like a tree planted by the rivers of water . . . and whatsoever he doeth shall prosper."

My prayer: Heavenly Father, I love you with all my heart. Thank you for your promise of prosperity and success. I will meditate upon your Word and do it, throughout the day.

Today's Scriptures: Ps. 1:1-3; Ps. 119:15; 1 Tim. 4:15.

December 20

Today God says, *"Your faith is the victory that overcomes the world."*

He promises me: "For whatsoever is born of God overcometh the world: and this is the victory that overcometh the world, even our faith" (1 John 5:4).

My response to the Word: Faith is the victory that overcomes the world. There are a thousand ways to please God, but not one of them works without faith. I want to please the Lord today; therefore, I will walk by faith, not by sight. I will live by faith. I will remember Jesus' words: "According to your faith be it unto you."

My prayer: Lord, thank you for the gift of faith. As I meditate upon your Word today, I know that my faith will build in my heart. I will walk by faith today.

Today's Scriptures: Matt. 9:29; Rom. 1:17; 2 Cor. 5:7.

December 21

Today God says, *"Have faith in Me."*

He promises me: "And Jesus answering saith unto them, Have faith in God. For verily I say unto you, That whosoever shall say unto this mountain, Be thou removed, and be thou cast into the sea; and shall not doubt in his heart, but shall believe that those things which he saith shall come to pass; he shall have whatsoever he saith" (Mark 11:22-23).

My response to the Word: God imparts faith to me through His Word. He commands me to have faith in Him. Therefore, I must absorb His Word at every opportunity. His Word builds mountain-moving faith in my heart. His Word imparts a faith that works. His Word tells me, "What things soever ye desire, when ye pray, believe that ye receive them, and ye shall have them."

My prayer: Lord, let the richness of your Word soak into me. I believe your promises and I will act accordingly throughout this day.

Today's Scriptures: Mark 11:24; Rom. 10:17; 1 John 5:4.

December 22

Today God says, *"With lovingkindness I have drawn you."*

He promises me: "The Lord hath appeared of old unto me, saying, Yea, I have loved thee with an everlasting love: therefore with lovingkindness I have drawn thee" (Jer. 31:3).

My response to the Word: God's lovingkindness is better than life to me. His love for me is everlasting. I will walk in the sunlight of His love throughout this day. Even when the sky is cloudy, I know that the sunlight shines above. By way of this analogy I will remember that God's love is always there as well, even when the clouds and storms of life appear threatening.

My prayer: Father, I receive your love. Your amazing, everlasting love truly is my life. Help me to fully know your love.

Today's Scriptures: Ps. 63:3; Ps. 92:2; Eph. 3:17.

December 23

Today God says, *"Your love for Me is better than any sacrifice."*

He promises me: "And to love him with all the heart, and with all the understanding, and with all the soul, and with all the strength, and to love his neighbour as himself, is more than all whole burnt offerings and sacrifices" (Mark 12:33).

My response to the Word: The theme of my life today will be: "And thou shalt love the Lord thy God with all thy heart, and with all thy soul, and with all thy mind, and with all thy strength: this is the first commandment. And the second is like, namely this, Thou shalt love thy neighbour as thyself. There is none other commandment greater than these."

My prayer: Lord, I will obey your Word through love, because I know that love is the fulfillment of your law. Let your love flow into me, through me, and out of me.

Today's Scriptures: Mark 12:30-31; John 14:15; Rom. 12:9.

December 24

Today God says, *"Jesus is the resurrection and the life."*

He promises me: "Jesus said unto her, I am the resurrection, and the life: he that believeth in me, though he were dead, yet shall he live: And whosoever liveth and believeth in me shall never die. Believest thou this?" (John 11:25-26).

My response to the Word: I believe that Jesus is the resurrection and the life. Because He lived, died, was buried, rose again, and ascended into heaven, I now know that I will not perish. My life will go on forever with Him in heaven. Faith is the key to this victory over death, as it is the key to victory in every area of life. I believe that I have eternal life through Jesus Christ, my Lord.

My prayer: Lord, thank you for the power of your resurrection that imparts eternal life to me. I believe in you with all my heart, and I thank you that I will never perish.

Today's Scriptures: Phil. 3:10; 1 Pet. 1:3; 1 Pet. 3:21.

December 25

Today God says, *"When you offer praise, you glorify Me."*

He promises me: "Whoso offereth praise glorifieth me: and to him that ordereth his conversation aright will I shew the salvation of God" (Ps. 50:23).

My response to the Word: Praising God is both practical and spiritual. It changes my focus away from the things of earth to the far-more-excellent things of heaven. It gives me emotional release. It cultivates the attitude of gratitude in my heart. It lifts me out of myself and above my problems. Most importantly, however, it glorifies my God.

My prayer: Lord God, I praise you, thank you, worship you, and adore you. You are everything to me. Throughout this day I want to glorify you in every possible way.

Today's Scriptures: Ps. 150; Jer. 20:13; Rev. 19:5-6.

December 26

Today God says, *"I will give you grace and glory."*

He promises me: "For the Lord God is a sun and shield: the Lord will give grace and glory: no good thing will he withhold from them that walk uprightly" (Ps. 84:11).

My response to the Word: God will not withhold any good things from me. He is my sun and my shield, and He promises to give me grace and glory. His amazing grace astounds me as I reflect upon His promise: "For thou, Lord, wilt bless the righteous; with favour wilt thou compass him as with a shield."

My prayer: Thank you, Father, for your loving grace. By faith, I will receive all that your grace offers me. May your grace and your glory rest upon me.

Today's Scriptures: Ps. 5:12; Rom. 3:24; Eph. 2:8-9.

December 27

Today God says, *"By finding Me you have found life, and I give you my favor."*

He promises me: "For whoso findeth me findeth life, and shall obtain favour of the Lord" (Prov. 8:35).

My response to the Word: Before I knew the Lord, I walked in death, not life. It was as though I was dead while alive. Now I am fully alive, and there is no death nor darkness within me at all. This is the Lord's favor at work in my life. Heaven has already begun its work in me. I am a citizen of the Kingdom of God, an emissary to this world of darkness. I will let my light shine in the darkness today.

My prayer: Lord, thank you for abundant and eternal life. Thank you for blessing me with your favor. I will serve you throughout this day.

Today's Scriptures: John 1:4; John 10:10; Col. 3:4.

December 28

Today God says, *"You are the temple of the Holy Spirit."*

He promises me: "What? know ye not that your body is the temple of the Holy Ghost which is in you, which ye have of God, and ye are not your own?" (1 Cor. 6:19).

My response to the Word: The indwelling life of the Spirit of God is my wellspring of power, love, and victory. I will be filled with God's Spirit, led by God's Spirit, and walk in the Spirit throughout this day, because I know this will lead to fruitfulness in my life. I will remember that my body is the temple of the Holy Spirit. Greater is He that is in me than he that is in the world.

My prayer: Thank you for the power of the Holy Spirit in my life, Father. He is my Teacher, Guide, Comforter, and life.

Today's Scriptures: Rom. 8:14; Eph. 5:18; Gal. 5:16; Gal. 5:22-23; 1 John 4:4.

December 29

Today God says, *"I will pour out My Spirit on all flesh."*

He promises me: "And it shall come to pass afterward, that I will pour out my spirit upon all flesh; and your sons and your daughters shall prophesy, your old men shall dream dreams, your young men shall see visions" (Joel 2:28).

My response to the Word: The last days, prophesied by so many of the Old Testament prophets, are upon us. Jesus foretold many of the events that are transpiring in our world today. One of the greatest things that will happen in the last days is the pouring out of God's Spirit upon all flesh. Throughout this day, I will pray for this end-time revival. It will be the greatest hour in all of human history.

My prayer: Father, I thank you that you have already revealed the end of the story in your Word. I know I have so many things to look forward to. May Jesus Christ return soon.

Today's Scriptures: Acts 1:8; Eph. 5:18; 1 John 4:2.

December 30

Today God says, *"Not one word of My promises has ever failed."*

He promises me: "Blessed be the Lord, that hath given rest unto his people Israel, according to all that he promised: there hath not failed one word of all his good promise, which he promised by the hand of Moses his servant" (1 Kings 8:56).

My response to the Word: God's good promises never fail. In fact, there is only one thing God cannot do, and that is fail. He is my faithful Father, and He promise to fulfill His Word in my life. "God is faithful, by whom ye were called unto the fellowship of his Son Jesus Christ our Lord" He promises, "My covenant will I not break, nor alter the thing that is gone out of my lips."

My prayer: Lord God, thank you for your great faithfulness in my life. I take my stand upon your promises, and I will walk in accord with them throughout this day.

Today's Scriptures: Ps. 89:34; 1 Cor. 1:9; 2 Pet. 1:4.

December 31

Today God says, *"Death and life are in the power of your tongue."*

He promises me: "Death and life are in the power of the tongue: and they that love it shall eat the fruit thereof" (Prov. 18:21).

My response to the Word: I will remember the power of my words throughout this day, and I will use my words sparingly and carefully. I want to speak truth at all times. I want my words to have life and minister grace to those who hear them. I know the truth of Jesus words: "For out of the abundance of the heart the mouth speaketh." Like the Psalmist, I want my mouth to speak wisdom and my heart to be full of understanding

My prayer: Heavenly Father, help me to speak words of life to myself and others. "May the words of my mouth, and the meditation of my heart, be acceptable in thy sight, O Lord, my strength, and my redeemer." Amen.

Today's Scriptures: Ps. 19:14; Ps. 49:3; Matt. 12:34; Eph. 4:29; James 3:6.

BIBLE PROMISES

SALVATION

For all have sinned, and come short of the glory of God. Romans 3:23

For the wages of sin is death; but the gift of God is eternal life through Jesus Christ our Lord. Romans 6:23

For God so loved the world, that he gave his only begotten Son, that whosoever believeth in him should not perish, but have everlasting life. John 3:16

But what saith it? The word is nigh thee, even in thy mouth, and in thy heart: that is, the word of faith, which we preach;
That if thou shalt confess with thy mouth the Lord Jesus, and shalt believe in thine heart that God hath raised him from the dead, thou shalt be saved.
For with the heart man believeth unto right-eousness; and with the mouth confession is made unto salvation. Romans 10:8-10

But as many as received him, to them gave he power to become the sons of God, even to them that believe on his name. John 1:12

SALVATION

And they said, Believe on the Lord Jesus Christ, and thou shalt be saved, and thy house. Acts 16:31

Therefore if any man be in Christ, he is a new creature: old things are passed away; behold, all things are become new. 2 Corinthians 5:17

Jesus answered and said unto him, Verily, verily, I say unto thee, Except a man be born again, he cannot see the kingdom of God. John 3:3

For if by one man's offence death reigned by one; much more they which receive abundance of grace and of the gift of righteousness shall reign in life by one, Jesus Christ. Romans 5:17

A new heart also will I give you, and a new spirit will I put within you: and I will take away the stony heart out of your flesh, and I will give you an heart of flesh.
And I will put my spirit within you, and cause you to walk in my statutes, and ye shall keep my judgments, and do them. Ezekiel 36:26-27

FAITH

For by grace are ye saved through faith; and that not of yourselves: it is the gift of God. Ephesians 2:8

I am crucified with Christ: nevertheless I live; yet not I, but Christ liveth in me: and the life which I now live in the flesh I live by the faith of the Son of God, who loved me, and gave himself for me. Galatians 2:20

For all the promises of God in him are yea, and in him Amen, unto the glory of God by us. 2 Corinthians 1:20

For therein is the righteousness of God revealed from faith to faith: as it is written, The just shall live by faith. Romans 1:17

So then faith cometh by hearing, and hearing by the word of God. Romans 10:17

Let us therefore come boldly unto the throne of grace, that we may obtain mercy, and find grace to help in time of need. Hebrews 4:16

The entrance of thy words giveth light; it giveth understanding unto the simple. Psalms 119:130

FAITH

But what saith it? The word is nigh thee, even in thy mouth, and in thy heart: that is, the word of faith, which we preach. Romans 10:8

For I say, through the grace given unto me, to every man that is among you, not to think of himself more highly than he ought to think; but to think soberly, according as God hath dealt to every man the measure of faith. Romans 12:3

But the fruit of the Spirit is love, joy, peace, longsuffering, gentleness, goodness, faith, Meekness, temperance: against such there is no law. Galatians 5:22-23

Now faith is the substance of things hoped for, the evidence of things not seen. Hebrews 11:1

But without faith it is impossible to please him: for he that cometh to God must believe that he is, and that he is a rewarder of them that diligently seek him. Hebrews 11:6

That ye be not slothful, but followers of them who through faith and patience inherit the promises. Hebrews 6:12

GOD'S WORD

*For as the rain cometh down, and the snow
from heaven, and returneth not thither, but
watereth the earth, and maketh it bring forth
and bud, that it may give seed to the sower,
and bread to the eater:*

*So shall my word be that goeth forth out of
my mouth: it shall not return unto me void,
but it shall accomplish that which I please,
and it shall prosper in the thing whereto I
sent it. Isaiah 55:10-11*

*Then said the Lord unto me, Thou hast well
seen: for I will hasten my word to perform it.
Jeremiah 1:12*

*Is not my word like as a fire? saith the Lord;
and like a hammer that breaketh the rock in
pieces? Jeremiah 23:29*

*Being born again, not of corruptible seed, but
of incorruptible, by the word of God, which
liveth and abideth for ever. 1 Peter 1:23*

*As newborn babes, desire the sincere milk of the
word, that ye may grow thereby. 1 Peter 2:2*

GOD'S WORD

For ever, O LORD, thy word is settled in heaven. Psalms 119:89

My son, attend to my words; incline thine ear unto my sayings.
Let them not depart from thine eyes; keep them in the midst of thine heart.
For they are life unto those that find them, and health to all their flesh. Proverbs 4:20-22

For the word of God is quick, and powerful, and sharper than any twoedged sword, piercing even to the dividing asunder of soul and spirit, and of the joints and marrow, and is a discerner of the thoughts and intents of the heart. Hebrews 4:12

And take the helmet of salvation, and the sword of the Spirit, which is the word of God. Ephesians 6:17

Bless the LORD, ye his angels, that excel in strength, that do his commandments, hearkening unto the voice of his word. Psalms 103:20

Thy word is a lamp unto my feet, and a light unto my path. Psalms 119:105

HEALTH AND HEALING

And said, If thou wilt diligently hearken to the voice of the LORD thy God, and wilt do that which is right in his sight, and wilt give ear to his commandments, and keep all his statutes, I will put none of these diseases upon thee, which I have brought upon the Egyptians: for I am the LORD that healeth thee. Exodus 15:26

And ye shall serve the LORD your God, and he shall bless thy bread, and thy water; and I will take sickness away from the midst of thee. Exodus 23:25

Is any sick among you? let him call for the elders of the church; and let them pray over him, anointing him with oil in the name of the Lord.
And the prayer of faith shall save the sick, and the Lord shall raise him up; and if he have committed sins, they shall be forgiven him. James 5:14-15

Who his own self bare our sins in his own body on the tree, that we, being dead to sins, should live unto righteousness: by whose stripes ye were healed. 1 Peter 2:24

HEALTH AND HEALING

That it might be fulfilled which was spoken by Esaias the prophet, saying, Himself took our infirmities, and bare our sicknesses.
Matthew 8:17

Jesus Christ the same yesterday, and to day, and for ever. Hebrews 13:8

Beloved, I wish above all things that thou mayest prosper and be in health, even as thy soul prospereth. 3 John 2

Bless the Lord, O my soul: and all that is within me, bless his holy name.

Bless the Lord, O my soul, and forget not all his benefits:

Who forgiveth all thine iniquities; who healeth all thy diseases;

Who redeemeth thy life from destruction; who crowneth thee with lovingkindness and tender mercies. Psalms 103:1-4

He sent his word, and healed them, and delivered them from their destructions.
Psalms 107:20

THE HOLY SPIRIT

But when the Comforter is come, whom I will send unto you from the Father, even the Spirit of truth, which proceedeth from the Father, he shall testify of me. John 15:26

And I say unto you, Ask, and it shall be given you; seek, and ye shall find; knock, and it shall be opened unto you.

For every one that asketh receiveth; and he that seeketh findeth; and to him that knocketh it shall be opened.

If ye then, being evil, know how to give good gifts unto your children: how much more shall your heavenly Father give the Holy Spirit to them that ask him? Luke 11:9-10, 13

But ye shall receive power, after that the Holy Ghost is come upon you: and ye shall be witnesses unto me both in Jerusalem, and in all Judaea, and in Samaria, and unto the uttermost part of the earth. Acts 1:8

But if the Spirit of him that raised up Jesus from the dead dwell in you, he that raised up

THE HOLY SPIRIT

Christ from the dead shall also quicken your mortal bodies by his Spirit that dwelleth in you. Romans 8:11

Howbeit when he, the Spirit of truth, is come, he will guide you into all truth: for he shall not speak of himself; but whatsoever he shall hear, that shall he speak: and he will show you things to come. John 16:13

Likewise the Spirit also helpeth our infirmities: for we know not what we should pray for as we ought: but the Spirit itself maketh intercession for us with groanings which cannot be uttered.

And he that searcheth the hearts knoweth what is the mind of the Spirit, because he maketh intercession for the saints according to the will of God. Romans 8:26-27

And because ye are sons, God hath sent forth the Spirit of his Son into your hearts, crying, Abba, Father. Galatians 4:6

PEACE

I will both lay me down in peace, and sleep: for thou, LORD, only makest me dwell in safety. Psalms 4:8

Mark the perfect man, and behold the upright: for the end of that man is peace. Psalms 37:37

Pray for the peace of Jerusalem: they shall prosper that love thee. Psalms 122:6

Thou wilt keep him in perfect peace, whose mind is stayed on thee: because he trusteth in thee. Isaiah 26:3

And the work of righteousness shall be peace; and the effect of righteousness quietness and assurance for ever. Isaiah 32:17

Peace I leave with you, my peace I give unto you: not as the world giveth, give I unto you. Let not your heart be troubled, neither let it be afraid. John 14:27

These things I have spoken unto you, that in me ye might have peace. In the world ye shall have tribulation: but be of good cheer; I have overcome the world. John 16:33

PEACE

Therefore being justified by faith, we have peace with God through our Lord Jesus Christ. Romans 5:1

Finally, brethren, farewell. Be perfect, be of good comfort, be of one mind, live in peace; and the God of love and peace shall be with you. 2 Corinthians 13:11

Be careful for nothing; but in every thing by prayer and supplication with thanksgiving let your requests be made known unto God.
And the peace of God, which passeth all understanding, shall keep your hearts and minds through Christ Jesus. Philippians 4:6-7

Now the Lord of peace himself give you peace always by all means. The Lord be with you all. 2 Thessalonians 3:16

The LORD will give strength unto his people; the LORD will bless his people with peace. Psalms 29:11

And the fruit of righteousness is sown in peace of them that make peace. James 3:18

PRAYER

If ye abide in me, and my words abide in you, ye shall ask what ye will, and it shall be done unto you. John 15:7

And in that day ye shall ask me nothing. Verily, verily, I say unto you, Whatsoever ye shall ask the Father in my name, he will give it you. John 16:23

Trust in the LORD with all thine heart; and lean not unto thine own understanding. In all thy ways acknowledge him, and he shall direct thy paths. Proverbs 3:5-6

Confess your faults one to another, and pray one for another, that ye may be healed. The effectual fervent prayer of a righteous man availeth much. James 5:16

And we know that all things work together for good to them that love God, to them who are the called according to his purpose. Romans 8:28

Again I say unto you, That if two of you shall agree on earth as touching any thing that they shall ask, it shall be done for them of my Father which is in heaven. Matthew 18:19

PRAYER

If I regard iniquity in my heart, the Lord will not hear me.

But verily God hath heard me; he hath attended to the voice of my prayer.

Blessed be God, which hath not turned away my prayer, nor his mercy from me. Psalms 66:18-20

And this is the confidence that we have in him, that, if we ask any thing according to his will, he heareth us:

And if we know that he hear us, whatsoever we ask, we know that we have the petitions that we desired of him. 1 John 5:14-15

Behold, the LORD's hand is not shortened, that it cannot save; neither his ear heavy, that it cannot hear. Isaiah 59:1

Call unto me, and I will answer thee, and show thee great and mighty things, which thou knowest not. Jeremiah 33:3

DIVINE PROTECTION

He that dwelleth in the secret place of the most High shall abide under the shadow of the Almighty.
I will say of the Lord, He is my refuge and my fortress: my God; in him will I trust.
Thou shalt not be afraid for the terror by night; nor for the arrow that flieth by day;
Nor for the pestilence that walketh in darkness; nor for the destruction that wasteth at noonday. Psalms 91:1-2, 5-6

But let all those that put their trust in thee rejoice: let them ever shout for joy, because thou defendest them: let them also that love thy name be joyful in thee.
For thou, Lord, wilt bless the righteous; with favour wilt thou compass him as with a shield. Psalms 5:11-12

The angel of the Lord encampeth round about them that fear him, and delivereth them. Psalms 34:7

Are not two sparrows sold for a farthing? and one of them shall not fall on the ground without your Father. Matthew 10:29

DIVINE PROTECTION

But the very hairs of your head are all numbered.

Fear ye not therefore, ye are of more value than many sparrows. Matthew 10:30-31

So shall they fear the name of the Lord from the west, and his glory from the rising of the sun. When the enemy shall come in like a flood, the Spirit of the Lord shall lift up a standard against him. Isaiah 59:19

For in the time of trouble he shall hide me in his pavilion: in the secret of his tabernacle shall he hide me; he shall set me up upon a rock. Psalms 27:5

No weapon that is formed against thee shall prosper; and every tongue that shall rise against thee in judgment thou shalt condemn. This is the heritage of the servants of the Lord, and their righteousness is of me, saith the Lord. Isaiah 54:17

In God have I put my trust: I will not be afraid what man can do unto me. Psalms 56:11

DIVINE PROVISION

Bring ye all the tithes into the storehouse, that there may be meat in mine house, and prove me now herewith, saith the Lord of hosts, if I will not open you the windows of heaven, and pour you out a blessing, that there shall not be room enough to receive it. Malachi 3:10

Give, and it shall be given unto you; good measure, pressed down, and shaken together, and running over, shall men give into your bosom. For with the same measure that ye mete withal it shall be measured to you again. Luke 6:38

Honour the Lord with thy substance, and with the firstfruits of all thine increase.
So shall thy barns be filled with plenty, and thy presses shall burst out with new wine. Proverbs 3:9

The young lions do lack, and suffer hunger: but they that seek the Lord shall not want any good thing. Psalms 34:10

DIVINE PROVISION

But this I say, He which soweth sparingly shall reap also sparingly; and he which soweth bountifully shall reap also bountifully.

Every man according as he purposeth in his heart, so let him give; not grudgingly, or of necessity: for God loveth a cheerful giver.
2 Corinthians 9:6

But my God shall supply all your need according to his riches in glory by Christ Jesus.
Philippians 4:19

But seek ye first the kingdom of God, and his righteousness; and all these things shall be added unto you. Matthew 6:33

Blessed is the man that walketh not in the counsel of the ungodly, nor standeth in the way of sinners, nor sitteth in the seat of the scornful.

But his delight is in the law of the Lord; and in his law doth he meditate day and night.

And he shall be like a tree planted by the rivers of water, that bringeth forth his fruit in his season; his leaf also shall not wither; and whatsoever he doeth shall prosper. Psalms 1:1-3

PERSONAL NOTES

BOOK ORDER FORM

Use this form to order additional books or for information about other inspirational books.

Book Title	Price	Quantity	Amount
Today God Says	$ 7.99	_____	$_____
God's Special Promises To Me	$ 9.99	_____	$_____
Prayers That Prevail	$ 9.99	_____	$_____
Prayers That Prevail for Your Children	$ 9.99	_____	$_____
Mini Prayers That Prevail	$ 5.99	_____	$_____

Shipping & Handling — Add $2.00 for the **first** book, **plus** $0.50 for **each** additional book. $_____

TOTAL ORDER AMOUNT — *Enclose check or money order. (No cash or C.O.D.'s.)* $_____

☐ Please send me information on other inspirational books.

☐ SPECIAL CHURCH DISCOUNT for orders of 50 or more call **1-800-262-2631**

Make check or money order payable to: **VICTORY HOUSE, INC.**
Mail order to: Victory House, Inc.
           P.O Box 700238
           Tulsa, OK 74170
Please print your name and address **clearly:**

Name _____

Address _____

City _____

State or Province _____

Zip or Postal Code _____

Telephone Number (____) _____

Foreign orders must be submitted by Credit Card only. Additional shipping costs will apply. Foreign orders are shipped by uninsured surface mail. We ship all orders within 48 hours of receipt of order.

MasterCard or VISA — For credit card orders you may use your MasterCard or VISA by completing the following information, or for **faster service,** call **1-800-262-2631**.

Card Name _____

Card Number _____

Expiration Date _____

Signature _____
                    (authorized signature)